From Schoole to School

changing scenes 1699 - 1999

Margaret Siddall

dh

Devonshire House

1999

Dedicated to 'St Martin's girls'
past, present and future

Cover illustrations: St Martin's girl today
looking back through time, Silwood House,
report card, homework timetable, gym
display, Hungerford Market House,
the original school uniform (back cover).

Published in 1999 by Devonshire House
Christow Devon EX6 7LU

British Library Cataloguing in Publication Data.
A catalogue record for this book
is available from the British Library.

ISBN 0 9524513 36

Printed and bound in Great Britain by
Lazarus Press
Caddsdown Bideford Devon EX39 3DX

Contents

	page
Illustrations	5
Pre-decimal money conversion	6
Foreword	7
The Legend of St Martin	8
Background	9

Chapters:

1. Beginnings 1699 - 1870	13
2. Charing Cross 1870 - 1928	35
3. Tulse Hill 1928 - 1939	57
4. War Years 1939 - 1945	81
5. Together Again 1945 - 1949	112
6. Widening Horizons 1949 - 1965	129
7. Adapting to Change 1965 - 1989	149
8. Towards the Future 1989 - 1999	176

School uniform price lists	208
Bibliography	209
Acknowledgements	210
Index	211

Illustrations

	page
Legend of St Martin and the beggar	8
Charity children lining the streets	20
Hungerford Market House, the original school	21
St Martin's in Charing Cross Road	36
Report card	54
View over the school field	59
The Duchess of York receiving a bouquet	64
Who's for tennis?	75
St Martin's at Tulse Hill	87
St John's playing field	95
Cast of *Quality Street*	117
Lined up on the top court	124
The old and the new 1699-1949	130
'Victorian' gymnastics display	135
St Martin's at leisure	138
The school cruise	160
Geography field trip	169
The disused swimming pool	183
Part of the school library	198
The Technology Centre	201

Pre-decimal money and conversion:

farthing = $^1/_{4d}$
halfpenny (ha'penny) = $^1/_{2d}$
1 penny = 1d
12 pence (d) = 1 shilling (s) = 5p
20 shillings = £1 = 100p
21 shillings = 1 guinea = £1.05

Foreword

Three years ago, Margaret Siddall wrote an autobiography of her childhood and wartime experiences, which included recollections of her days at St Martin-in-the-Fields High School. To celebrate the school's tercentenary, her latest book gives a fascinating insight into the development of education in this country from 1699 to 1999.

The book contains photographs and extracts from school magazines and newsletters and minutes of meetings. These, together with quotes from staff and pupils, past and present, give a vivid and real picture of how life at St Martin-in-the-Fields High School for Girls has changed and developed since its early years.

The school started out as a Charity School and changed to an Endowed Grammar School in the late 1800s. After the second world war, when my father Clement Attlee was Prime Minister and deeply involved with educational policies, the school retained its Direct Grant status until it became Comprehensive in 1977.

I have known Margaret both as a colleague and friend for over 35 years. In the early 1970s she was one of my nursery assistants at a small independent pre-prep school where I was headmistress. Although she had no formal training, she has always had a wonderful gift with children and a great interest in education and learning.

Her delightful book brings to life the story of education over three centuries through the history of St Martin-in-the-Fields School.

Lady Felicity Harwood 1998

The School Song
—The Legend of St Martin

St Martin through the fields did pass,
When snow lay white one Candlemas,
And saw a poor man, lean and old,
Half naked in the bitter cold.
His heart was pierced with pity's pain,
He cut his duffle cloak in twain
And clothed that beggar to his gain,
St Martin, in the fields.

Now where St Martin's shrine doth stand,
All in the fields beside the Strand.
The gift he gave has spread so wide
That all who come find warmth inside.
And London's poor and needy folk,
Find shelter 'neath St Martin's cloak,
Find warmth and shelter 'neath his cloak,
St Martin-in-the-Fields.

And o'er our school his cloak doth spread,
To shelter many a childish head.
Our school where games and learning ride
In joyous laughter side by side.
From here into the world we'll fare,
The wrong to fight, the right to dare,
Remembering whose cloak we wear,
St Martin-in-the-Fields.

The legend of St Martin and the beggar
(Brenda Cady School magazine 1954)

Verses one and two by
Miss M. Anne Richmond
Verse three and music by
Miss D. Copland

8

Background

From the unmistakable shrill sounds of children in a country playground, to groups clustered around museum exhibits, *school* is everywhere. But today's multi-media workshops, modern laboratories and increasing use of the Internet have moved education a long way from the time when writing was considered an extra subject.

By tracing the eventful history of one London school, St Martin-in-the-Fields, a fascinating picture emerges of how education in England has developed. St Martin's is 300 years old, and to celebrate the tercentenary *From Schoole to School: changing scenes 1699-1999* shows how the tentative beginnings of a simple charity school have successfully adapted to changing times.

To fill in the background: there had been song schools, where any teaching was through singing and chanting. There were dame schools, some no more than child-minding facilities in the minder's home as she coped with her washing and cooking, although basic reading and counting were sometimes taught. Chantry schools had sprung up, too, where teaching was fitted in with the priest's duties of praying for the dead. And from time to time, wealthy merchants had set up endowed grammar schools for boys, to give a grounding in Latin.

For the very poor, apprentice schools, 'nunnery' schools, petty schools, ABC schools and orphanage schools, known as hospitals, had all existed, giving limited reading and number work. Schools attached to workhouses enabled more poor children to gain a basic knowledge of reading, and by the mid 17th century non-conformist 'dissenter' schools came into being. But provision was fragmented partly due to political, religious and economic tensions — and the fear of an educated society.

In 1695, in his book *Some Thoughts Concerning Education*, John Locke helped expand a rising interest in education when he said, 'true education is a conditioning of the mind rather than the acquisition of factual knowledge'. He believed that learning should be based on activity and curiosity rather than rule and rote. Yet, despite this advanced thinking, weaving, spinning, sewing and similar household tasks continued to be more important for girls, as it was not thought appropriate for girls to have the same education as boys. Even so, his book highlighted the need for more widespread schooling, and soon after publication the charity school movement started.

Set up in 1698, one of the founders was the Society for Promoting Christian Knowledge (SPCK), and it was this organisation which laid the foundations for St Martin-in-the-Fields High School. The aims of the SPCK were to promote:

> 'The Knowledge and Practice of the Christian Religion as Professed and Taught in the Church of England and for teaching such other things as are most suitable for their [charity children] condition.'

The Society gave advice, organised schemes for raising money and often found suitable teachers. Their guide lines stated that children had to be between seven and twelve years old and their parents too poor to afford any other form of education. A register was to be called each morning and afternoon, and truants could be expelled. The schools' duties were to teach the children the catechism, good manners and behaviour and 'to prevent lying, cursing and profanity of the Lord's day'.

To fund the charity schools, the SPCK established the tradition of a central body of local trustees. It was intended that schools should not just be supported by a few wealthy founders as before; instead the whole parish would be included. In this way shopkeepers and tradesmen became involved with their own local school by taking an interest in its success and funding.

Collections were made at churches and chapels, and statuettes of charity children with collecting boxes were later placed outside church doors. With donations, legacies and promised annual subscriptions, money was raised to found and maintain many new schools. Although the purpose was primarily to provide 'moral discipline and religious principles for the children of the poor', the result meant more children would be able to have some sort of education. And so, in 1699, St Martin's School was founded.

In September 1943, when as a shy eight-year-old I started at St Martin's, I bought a much-treasured book called *A Short History of St Martin-in-the-Fields High School for Girls*. It was written by the then senior history mistress and deputy head, Miss D.H. Thomas. In her preface, Miss Thomas described the old minute books, which go back to the founding of the school and give the fascinating details on which her book is based.

The original spelling, not yet standardised, and use of capital letters were retained by Miss Thomas, and these I have used in the many quotations in the first two chapters of the present book.

In the early days, when both boys and girls went to St Martin's they were mostly kept separate, although the two sections were one school administered by the same trustees. For clarity, I have concentrated on the girls' section, but much would have been similar for the boys.

Another excellent source of reference has been the school magazines, with articles written by girls and staff from 1922 to 1983. These accounts not only give a unique description of what was happening, but bring out the minor details which are so easily forgotten. The magazines have been described as 'living, contemporary history', and as such they, and the newsletters that followed them, have been invaluable. I much appreciate the school's permission to use this material and illustrations from the magazines and archives.

Many people have kindly contributed stories and anecdotes, too, some of which go back more than half a century. Most writers said how much they had enjoyed 'indulging in nostalgia' and that 'memories came tumbling out'. Their memories have now tumbled into shape to help create a first-hand picture of the school's 'modern' era.

The everyday hard work of any school is recorded in lists of examination results, but they cannot show the wider interests that help prepare children for life. Details of the many visits, talks, clubs and societies, as well as money-raising events and charities to which St Martin's subscribed, show the involvement and interest gained through these experiences. Opportunities for individual initiative abound, and over the years wider activities have worked for the good of pupils, school and the community.

One regret I have is in not making the most of my own school days. In fact I was once described as an 'also ran'. But education is a continuing process and St Martin's taught me *how* to learn, which later enabled me to take university courses as a 'mature student'. Several of my contemporaries who, like me, had their education disrupted by the war, have studied in later years, too, because of the firm foundations gained at St Martin's.

Today, Old Girls' comments reinforce the feeling of a 'happy, caring school', with expressions of gratitude for the discipline, confidence in oneself and the 'sheer quality of teaching'. One Old Girl summed up these feelings by saying, 'I am an old St Martin's girl and proud of it!'

To bring this picture of school life right up to date, the present headteacher, Mrs Lesley Morrison, shows St Martin's as a forward-looking community, overcoming new demands in a multi-cultural and technological age.

My special thanks to staff and girls, past and present, for helping this project to come alive.

Margaret Siddall (née Green, St Martin's 1943-1952)
Christow, Devon
1999

Note: A complete list of contributors and those who have given back-ground material can be found at the end of the book.

1. Beginnings: 1699-1870

A stream of laughing, exuberant girls poured through the wide gateway and spilled on to the pavement in a surge of dark brown school uniforms. The stream spread out as some girls crossed the busy road. Others moved off in both directions, walking down Tulse Hill, singly or in chattering groups. A red double-decker bus pulled up at the kerb, temporarily blocking the traffic while more brown-clad girls crowded inside.

This could have been any throng of schoolgirls, hurrying home after a busy day working through the National Curriculum. But these were St Martin's girls, with a pride in the school's long tradition and the knowledge that once, many years ago, their school had been in the centre of London, when only an occasional horse and cart clattered by over the cobbled street.

Few girls went to school then, and for those who did, their learning was basic, with no career prospects or independent life ahead. Today's structured, technological approach and excitement of the Internet would have been unimaginable. Looking back through changing times, to an age when most children had no schooling and teachers were untrained, a vastly different picture of school life emerges.

*   *   *   *

'Writing a very good hand and understanding knitting and plane work' were some of the qualifications needed for the first headmistress of what was to become St Martin-in-the-Fields High School.

The tentative foundations were laid in 1699, when schooling was a haphazard affair and mostly for boys. In May that year, an appeal went out to parishioners for subscriptions and donations to start a parochial charity school in the Strand. So successful was it that enough money was raised to hire a large room in Hungerford Market House, nearby, formerly used by French Huguenots as a church. The room was furnished with benches and St Martin's School was opened for fifty poor boys.

By the 6th of January 1700 a further £15.16s had been 'gather'd in St Martin's parish', so it was agreed that the school should be extended to take up to forty poor girls in 'a very convenient place in Castle St. near Leicester Fields' (Leicester Square). Mrs Mary Harbin from 'ye sign of the Coffee Mill and Sugar Loafe in St James Street' was duly appointed as schoolmistress, with a salary of £24 a year and 'the conveniency of a lodging'.

The building was approved by the vicar of St Martin-in-the-Fields Church, the Reverend Dr Lancaster, and acquired early in February at an annual rent of six guineas. The SPCK minutes for the 3rd of February mentioned the twenty girls 'cloathed at St Martin-in-the-Fields', and the school reported that this section opened on Monday the 10th of February.

Twelve spelling books and twelve psalters were initially provided. 'Cyphering' books and thirty *Expositions of the Church Catechism* were also bought. Later came copies of *The Whole Duty of Man*, which featured prominently in these early days of charity schools. Costs were meticulously recorded in the minute books including: ten shillings for a grate, fender, shovel and poker; three shillings and sixpence for account and receipt books; and one shilling and a penny for paper, ink, standish and sand box — a standish being a stand and dish for pen and ink, while sand was used for drying the ink.

At that time, school buildings usually consisted of one large room or barn-shaped building, with a room attached for the schoolmaster or mistress. Here, different ages would be occupied with their appointed tasks of chanting the alphabet, reading, sewing or occasionally writing on slates.

The masters and mistresses were instructed to take the children to church twice on Sundays and holy days, and to teach them to join in the services and behave reverently. Prayers were to be said in school each morning and before going home, and grace said before and after meals. Besides learning to read and knit, girls would be taught to sew and make and mend their own clothes.

An essential part of the charity school scheme was to make sure the children were well clothed, so where funds allowed, a distinctive uniform was to be provided. This provision was partly because children would have gone to school in their ragged clothes, and partly so that the charity school children could be easily recognised in their cloaks of red, blue, green or grey. It was also said that the children could then be reminded of their 'servile state as public objects of charity'. This accepted belief of the time was to make sure that charity children would 'know their station in life and how mean their circumstances'.

Rules for London charity schools said:

> 'When the children are cloathed they wear their caps, bands and cloaths every day; whereby the Trustees, Benefactors and others may know and see what their behaviour is abroad.'

For St Martin's children, care was taken with their clothing throughout the early days while it was provided.

Mr Honnour, the shoemaker, was 'order'd to measure and make shoes of good calves leather' at two shillings a pair. Quoifs and handkerchiefs for twenty girls were needed, and the tailor was instructed to make their gowns. But the parents had to make the petticoats from 'Blew half thick'.

Eighteen pairs of gloves were bought for five shillings and ninepence, and twenty-one pairs of woollen stockings cost fifteen shillings. Later, orange-coloured yarn was bought so that the gloves and stockings could be knitted by the schoolmistress or the girls themselves. Thus each girl was issued with:

> 'A gown and Petticoat, one Cap, one Band, one pair of Stockins and one pair of Shoes.'

The gown and 'stockins' were only to be worn on 'Sundays, Holy days and such Wednesdays as they go to Trinity Chappell to hear the Sermon'. The following day they were to be returned to the school to be 'laid up', and Mrs Harbin was ordered to take care to have the gowns 'turn'd upside down'.

Money for funding continued to be collected over the years and minutes refer to collections being made at Trinity Chapel, Oxendon Chappell, Russell Court Chappelle and later at Spring Gardens and Tavistock Chapels. Special collections also came from the parish church of St Martin, where monthly lectures or sermons were given by outside speakers who were paid between two shillings and sixpence and ten shillings for their lecture.

Once a month the schoolmistress had to report to the board of trustees:

> 'In relation to the behaviour of the Girls in their Manners, wearing of their Cloaths etc., absence from school.'

And each week two trustees in their tall top hats visited the school to observe its progress. The girls sat on wooden forms around the edge of the bare room, some in turn laboriously reading the bible or catechism to the schoolmistress, others occupied with sewing or silent reading.

School started at 7 o'clock in summertime and the morning session finished at 11, but in winter the children were allowed to start an hour later. There was then a break until 1 o'clock, when they returned for the afternoon. In summer they finished at 5 o'clock, and 4 in winter when they hurried back to their houses through the darkening streets, leaving the mistress in the empty school with her coal fire and flickering candle.

For 'Encouragement in such matters as she shall think fit', the trustees agreed that Mrs Harbin should be given three shillings to be distributed to the girls. At the same meeting, reporting on the girls 'Proficiencies and their learning and Catechism', several girls were found to be 'very forward in their learning'. So much so that the committee agreed to 'consider next meeting whether it be proper to learn the girls to write'. Usually, writing was seldom considered until most children could read competently.

As a result, a ream of paper was ordered, together with pens, ink and another standish. The following year more paper was bought, and copy books were made in which the schoolmistress wrote neatly formed letters and words or didactic sentences, to be carefully copied underneath. Mrs Harbin was allowed an extra five pounds a year for teaching the girls to write, so writing was established and the children's proficiency judged once a quarter. Only the boys were taught arithmetic, because this was regarded as a 'superior accomplishment' which would be of little use to girls.

By 1704 the girls' section of the school had increased by ten, overcrowding the small classroom, so new premises were soon found in Hunt's Court, Castle Street (St Martin's Lane). But as the roof was too low, alterations were quickly put in hand to raise it. Mrs Harbin moved with the school where once again she lived in, and her valuable services for her 'extraordinary care and diligence in teaching the Girlls and makeing the Childrens Linnen and Stockings' were later recorded by a presentation of two guineas.

The following year, the annual report of the SPCK, on charity schools in London and Westminster, stated that St Martin-in-the-Fields taught and clothed eighty boys and fifty girls and that twenty-four boys and four girls had been 'put out apprentices from the beginning'.

Apprenticeships were generally found for the children after they were 'sufficiently instructed and duly qualified' to leave school. Most girls went into domestic service in a large house or became seamstresses, although both boys and girls could be apprenticed to learn a trade, such as bridle or cork cutters, gingerbread baker, or makers of snuffboxes, garters, mantuas (ladies' gowns or mantles) or perukes (wigs).

New apprentices were each given a bible and copy book when they left the school, and forty shillings for clothing provided their school clothes and any badges had been returned. *The Whole Duty of Man* was also given to them after a legacy from a parishioner had been left for this purpose.

The trustees appeared to take great care in finding suitable apprenticeships, and after the prospective employer's character was approved, an apprentice went for a month to testify 'their good liking of each other'. If, after a month, the trustees considered the work unsuitable another apprenticeship was sought. The consideration shown by St Martin's trustees did not reflect the attitude of all schools. St Martin's children were lucky.

Despite moving to a building with nearly twice the annual rent, in 1707 the trustees had received sufficient money from donations, subscriptions and legacies to invest £200. Further investments were made in 1708 when the minutes recorded, '. . . there being an oppertunity of placeing out 120 lb. uppon Land Security'.

Having settled down in the larger building in Hunt's Court, the school continued to flourish under the care of Mrs Harbin. A clock was bought when the school was offered 'an indifferent good one for forty shillings'. And five shillings was regularly paid to a Mr Hammers for 'a Years Keeping the Clock'.

Once a year each child was given a complete set of new clothes, ready for the Whitsun procession of charity schools. The annual distribution of clothes continued for many years as a later minute showed:

> 'Several of the House Girls [are] in great want of Bodice, order'd that 40 pair of Leathern ones be made to supply the present Necessity and the next Whitsuntides Clothing.'

The Whitsun procession was suggested by the SPCK, who arranged for charity schools in the London area to walk to church for a special service.

The first procession had been in 1704 to St Andrew's Church, Holborn, but the venue proved too small, as in successive years the number of charity children increased. The event became a highlight of the year, and children who had left school to be apprenticed were also included.

At 8 o'clock in the morning, led by the trustees, the long line of

St Martin's children set off in pairs, 'all new cloathed against Whitsuntide'. They walked along the cobbled streets to St Sepulchre's Church, where a sermon was preached to encourage donations from the parish. The children sat on display in their new clothes and bright yellow mittens and ribbons to soften the hearts of the congregation.

Not only were new clothes bought, but when the children returned from the procession they were allowed a special dinner 'provided the same did not exceed 6d each child'. On one occasion they were given:

> '3 ounces of gingerbread before going to Church, and three quarters of plumb-cake, with 4oz of cheese at their returne back.'

On another occasion a barrel of beer was ordered for the children, at ten shillings a barrel. Beer was a regular part of the meal after the Whitsun procession, and this continued for many years. But one year the Ladies' Committee pointed out to the trustees that the children's beer was 'hardly good enough for them'.

In July 1713, as well as the Whitsun procession, charity schools in and around London joined in the public thanksgiving for the Treaty of Utrecht after the Spanish War of Succession. The event was an enormous affair, with 4,000 charity children perched on specially erected scaffolding. Thousands of people also lined the streets to watch the procession of horse-drawn carriages clattering by. Afterwards, under the care of the dedicated Mrs Harbin and the boys' schoolmaster, the children from St Martin's walked in line to St Paul's Cathedral for the thanksgiving service.

Discipline was firmly maintained both in and out of school, when that same year a book was bought to record the names of children for frequent misdemeanours:

> 'All that have bin twice complained of by the Master, Mistress and others shall have their names writ in the book for that purpose and called Dooms-Day Book.'

19

Charity children lining the streets (SPCK)

If a second offence occurred, and the offender's name was found in the book, the boy or girl was immediately expelled. One girl was discharged from school for having been absent for two months and for being *incorrigible* — but her incorrigibility wasn't explained.

Mrs Harbin may well have continued at the school for many more years, but for an unfortunate incident which resulted in 'Complaint haveing been made to the Trustees by severall Subscribers and others'. Her offence was not praying in school for King George 1 and she admitted 'her unhappiness in not being capable, with the sattisfaction of her owne mind, to take the oaths the law requires'. Because of her Jacobite leanings, Mrs Harbin, after years of dedication to the school, resigned, with the regret of the trustees and a good testimonial:

> 'This is to Certifie whom it may concern, That Mary Harbin, late Mistress of the Charity Schoole for poor girlls in the parish of St Martin in the Fields in the City and Liberty of Westminster was not dismist from the said employment, for any inabillity, or neglect in discharge of the same, being Admirably Qualified and every way capacitated . . .'

Mrs Mary Worthrington, a widow, succeeded Mrs Harbin after the greatest care was taken to ensure her suitability. Several prospective candidates were interviewed individually and 'Interrogated as to their Principles and Qualifications'.

Beyond the confines of St Martin's, educating children was becoming more accepted, although there were still many dissenting voices over the value of educating the poor. An increasing number felt children should use their time more profitably; thus came a rise in the number of industrial and workhouse schools where trades were being taught. Because of this, the SPCK wrote to the trustees of each charity school urging them to add:

> '. . .some kind of labour to the Instruction given to children, this will bring them to the Habit of Industry . . . and effectively obviate any Objections against Charity Schools . . .'

For some time, St Martin's trustees had been discussing a proposal to extend the school to include orphans, as other neighbouring charity schools were doing. So in 1718 a seven-year lease was signed for the upper floor of Hungerford Market House, the original building for the boys' section. Thirty 'poor unhappy orphans' were taken in, having been 'exposed to the contagion of bad example, unwholesome diett and hard usage'.

The overall number of children was augmented, from time to time, by the addition of names contained in *The Orphan's booke*. A matron was appointed to look after the boarders and this boarding part of the school remained for many years. The parish paid eight shillings a month for each boy and girl for maintenance, *Hungerford Market House, the original school (School archives)* clothing and teaching, and with this merging of voluntary and rate-aided funding, gradually there began a blurring of roles for different types of school.

21

Unfortunately, the death of Mrs Worthrington in 1723 meant further interviews were needed to find a successor, and this time another widow, Mrs Isabella Hamers, was appointed. Mrs Hamers was 'about 42 years old' and had two boys 'both from her'. Her qualifications were that she:

> 'Understands the English tongue, writes a plain and legible hand, has taught plain works and is mistress of her needle and knitting.'

Mrs Hamers was not only the schoolmistress but was to live in and look after the twenty girl boarders, both in and out of school hours. Despite this rigorous routine she remained for thirteen years.

During this time the General Workhouse Act was passed, increasing the number of workhouses. A schoolmaster was often engaged to teach the children reading and possibly some writing, together with the main occupations of spinning, weaving and knitting. In this way it was hoped that the children of the poor would grow up with 'habits of virtue and be inured to labour', instead of being 'bred in ignorance and vice to an idle, beggarly and vagabond life'. Other children were apprenticed from an early age to costermongers, chimney sweeps or pedlars, so children who had been accepted by a charity school, such as St Martin's, were fortunate by comparison.

The old church of St Martin was to be replaced by a magnificent new building, designed by architect Sir James Gibbs, a pupil of Sir Christopher Wren. The gleaming white building, which rose up with a contemporary spire above a mock Greek pillared portico, was both admired and ridiculed because of the different styles. The church was finished in 1726 and had a special box high up in the west end for the charity children.

The need for charity schools was constantly emphasised, so that donations and subscriptions would continue. Many of these had been handed in at church or chapel services, but a report in the school minutes instructed that:

> 'No Fees or Money be henceforth given, at any Collections for these Schooles, to the Clerks, Sextons, Beadles, the Vestry or Pew Keepers at Church or Chappells. Order'd The Thanks of the Trustees for the same.'

A later order said:

> 'A Copper Plate be provided with a proper blank Receipt graved thereon; & that such a Receipt be delivered to each Subscriber on the Payment of their Subscription.'

Mrs Hamers' successor, Mrs Joyce Green, was asked to resign after less than two years because of 'being married, her ill state of Health & Neglect of the School'. Her husband was summoned to the trustees and told that, 'It was not thought proper she should be continued any Longer School Mistress'.

Two candidates emerged for the vacant post, and a Mrs Baldwin was successful. Mrs Baldwin lived in as before and was allowed 'Coals and Candles with soap to wash her own wearing Linen'. The second candidate at that time was Mrs Sarah Bowen, who took over from Mrs Baldwin in 1753.

Mrs Bowen was the wife of the schoolmaster, Tempest Bowen, which may have been the reason for her appointment. It was unusual for married women to be schoolmistresses, as the unmarried or widowed were considered more suitable. Because of joint living arrangements Mr and Mrs Bowen shared the concession of candles and coal, and Mrs Bowen was allowed an extra £15 a year as she was 'Dieted at the Expence of her Husband'.

Mrs Bowen remained in the post until 1766, even though a new schoolmaster for the boys' section had been appointed in 1759, when the master's separate quarters and the concessions of two chaldrons of coal and five dozen candles were reinstated. Mrs Sarah Maskall succeeded Mrs Bowen and stayed for over seven years.

From November 1773, the children started school at 8.30 instead of 8, and the morning session continued until 12 o'clock. They had to return again punctually at 1.30, and during the winter, stay in school until it was dark. The length of teaching time remained the same, but living in and being constantly in charge of the girls put a great strain on the schoolmistresses. A month later, Mrs Maskall resigned because of her 'Health having for some Time past been but very indifferent'.

The schoolmasters also suffered from health problems and it was minuted that:

> 'In the case of sickness it is hereby order'd that he [the master] appoint a senior boy in his stead to give account of misbehaviour in Church'.

Later, two senior boys — who may have been no more than ten or eleven years old — were to give account of the misbehaviour of the rest of the boys during the master's absence, when he was allowed to miss early prayers in church during his illness.

The new schoolmistress, Mrs Elizabeth Hart, fared no better than her predecessors, and after only two years her health was 'much impaired by her constant and due attendance upon the Duty of her office'. Mrs Hart's hours were reduced, and her salary accordingly, when Mrs Anne Tilton became her assistant. Alas, after going into the country for a month because of her ill state of health, Mrs Hart died. Mrs Tilton took over and stayed with the school for the next seventeen years.

Over the years, with successive masters and mistresses, the school gained in strength. Collections and subscriptions continued to be received, and some of the everyday running expenses of the school were now met by interest on investments. A regular collection was made when the children had their quarterly examinations, and unknown benefactors gave two Queen Anne five guinea and two half guineas pieces.

Legacies were another source of income and these varied from 'forty shillings per annum for ever', to several of £500. A painting of 'Francis Caryl Esq.', who had donated £500, was presented to the school on his death, and the picture was to become a constant link with the past. Some wills instructed how the money was to be spent, such as 'shifts' for the girls and copies of *The Whole Duty of Man*.

Another benefactor, Sir John Taylor, specified that the boys should attend his funeral and that 'one guinea be given each boy for his trouble'. His son, Michael Angelo Taylor, 'in his great Liberality' sent a further thirty-nine guineas, one for each of the girls. When the boys and girls received their guinea they were:

> 'Admonished by the Chairman. . .to behave themselves respectfully to the Trustees & Inhabitants of this Parish in particular and the Publick in general.'

A legacy of £1,000, which was left jointly between St Martin's, St Dunstan's and St Clement's schools, was used to buy the ground rents of seven houses in Belton Street, to provide a small but regular income. A box was bought to keep:

> 'the writings of the said Purchace in, having 3 keys, one for each school, And the Box to be kept in St Martin's Library.'

Misdemeanours and incorrigible behaviour continued and the miscreants were duly punished. One girl was sent home for the misbehaviour of her mother, but after the mother had admitted her wrong doing the girl was re-instated. Any boy who played truant had to wear a specially made coat with yellow sleeves and a 'slip of yellow' down the back seam. The boy could be made to wear the coat for any offence the board of trustees felt deserved this punishment.

One activity the children looked forward to was beating the bounds. On the Tuesday before the charity procession the girls went straight to the church, while the boys joined the Beadle and clergy to walk the principal streets beating the boundary stones of the parish with long canes:

> '. . .in order to make Perambulations & Processions round the said parish for Viewing & Considering the ancient Bounds & Limits to prevent Incroachment & Contentions.'

But contrasting with this ancient ritual, the early years of the Industrial Revolution were starting to take effect.

More children were now being employed in factories, which were using steam-driven machinery, producing greater output through greater speed. Some factories continued to provide minimal opportunities for learning, even so there were still many children who were not receiving even the simplest education.

By 1776 St Martin's was once more out-growing its buildings, and it was agreed not to continue the lease on Hungerford Market

House when it next came up for renewal. Much discussion and searching took place to find a new building, and although suitable sites were seen, nothing came of them. One house in St Martin's Lane appeared so suitable that the trustees agreed to double their subscriptions to help defray the cost. However, the proposal was dropped after a petition signed by thirty-eight neighbours objected to the house becoming:

> '. . .a Charity School of St Martin in the Fields, being well assured any such school would be attended with great inconvenience to the Neighbourhood'.

Despite this attitude, most of the time communities were keen to help their charity schools, and interest was not only shown by donating money. One resident of Wardour Street wrote to say:

> 'I offer. . .to the trustees of the Charity School of St Martin in the Fields for their approbation annually to present. . .Two Silver Medals as Premium for the best performance in writing. . .one for the boys, the other for the girls.'

The medals were to be worn on 'walking days' and every Sunday until the next successful candidate received them.

Sundays were special days for the children who lived in, because Sundays started with bread and butter and beer. For the rest of the week breakfast alternated between water gruel, broth and milk. The Sunday midday dinner was roast beef and *roots*, while on Tuesdays and Thursdays the meat was boiled. On other days the children had rice pudding, 'plumb' pudding or suet pudding, and for supper each evening there was bread and cheese.

The cook was instructed to go to market in the morning to 'chuse and see her meat weigh'd' and 'no stale joints nor pieces to be Received'. Shoulder and leg of mutton were acceptable, but salted meat, and breast, neck and brisket of beef had to be *refus'd*.

After the disappointment of the house in St Martin's Lane, a further five years went by before negotiations were started for a house in George Street. The building was old and proved to be in need of many repairs, but here the school stayed for the next twelve years.

In 1793, while still in George Street, Mrs Tilton:

'. . . begged leave to resign her Office; finding herself from her State of Health unable longer to continue in the same to do the Duties thereof with Credit to herself or Justice to the Charity.'

This time advertisements were placed in *The Daily Advertiser, The Times* and *Morning Herald*:

St Martin in the Fields

'Wanted as Mistress of the Charity School in this Parish a sober, decent, well-behaved unmarried Woman turned of thirty years of Age qualified to instruct about 40 Girls in Reading, Plain-Work & Knitting, careful & attentive to the Morals & Conduct of the Children committed to her Care, of a proper economical Turn as the Children are lodged and boarded in the School-House where the Mistress will be expected constantly to reside with the Assistance of a Servant and the Older Children to conduct the Business of the House. . .'

Twelve of the twenty-three applicants appeared to be eligible, and after a vote was taken by the trustees, Mrs Elizabeth Sedgewick was the successful candidate. But sadly her death two years later resulted in the advertisement being re-inserted in the newspapers. This time, Mrs Martha Gold was appointed, with a salary of £25 a year.

By now, the old house in George Street had become even more dilapidated and a new building was once again urgently sought. As a suitable one could not be found, the trustees agreed that a new school should be purpose built in Heming's Row (St Martin's Place).

The old houses were to be sold 'with all possible speed', when in June 1796 the foundation stone for the new building was laid by the vicar of St Martin-in-the-Fields, the Reverend Dr Hamilton. After the ceremony the children were 'very plentifully served with Roast Beef and Plumb Pudding'. The following year the new school building was ready to be furnished. Twenty iron bedsteads, mattresses, bolsters and rugs were ordered, together with a 'beech bedstead' for the matron from Mr Chippendale, whose family workshop was nearby in St Martin's Lane.

With the new building came the end of the first century of St Martin's charity school, which had seen many changes both socially and educationally. The once decreasing population was growing, due to better health through improved medical services, and towns were starting to expand.

Charity and philanthropy had pin-pointed the need to teach children to read, and from this, wider educational provision spread. But absenteeism was a major problem, often because of epidemics of measles, whooping cough or scarlet fever sweeping through the school, or sometimes for a simple thing like chilblains preventing children from wearing their boots.

As 80% of children still did not go to school, child labour, appalling poverty and child crime became major social problems. Response to these problems broadened the desire to educate children not just through existing, mostly religious, organisations, but through wider channels. Industrial schools became more numerous, although learning to spin and weave were still seen as more important than reading.

Although older children had always helped with younger ones, the rise of the monitorial system provided many more school places, by enabling large groups to be taught by a monitor in a more organised way. A later development was the system of 'pupil-teachers', who would be examined after supervised training.

The rival organisations of Quaker Lancastrians, which became the British and Foreign School Society, and the Church of England's 'National Society for Promoting the Education of the Poor in accordance with the Principles of the Established Church' (the National Society), spread almost identical monitorial systems throughout the country.

The National Society emerged as the larger of these two organisations and gradually began to take over many of the schools which the SPCK had helped to start. At the same time the first parliamentary committee was set up to consider education. In 1833, through the Committee of Council for Education, the government gave grants to both the National Society and the British and Foreign Society, and government inspectors were appointed to supervise education in their schools. Thus the pattern was set for state involvement.

The start of infant and kindergarten schools, though small, had a lasting influence on education, too. The emphasis on teaching 'not by severity but by kindness' was the essence of the nationwide Infant School Society.

Through all this educational expansion, St Martin's carried on in its purpose-built school in Heming's Row. Arithmetic had been added to the curriculum for the girls, and Mrs McCleary, the schoolmistress, took over its teaching from a Mr Wilson. Two years later, in 1835, extra remuneration was suggested for doing so; and writing was still considered an extra subject that warranted further payment.

The domestic problem of new ribbons for the girls' caps cropped up, when it was suggested by the Ladies' Committee that new ones were bought to match the 'frocks' as the original colour was too conspicuous. The same year, cloaks were needed and *lawn* for *tippets*. On the death of King William, in 1837, 'new mourning' was bought for the children, so once again 'newly clothed' they lined the streets in orderly fashion, this time to watch the funeral cortège go by.

A further development, beyond St Martin's, was the founding of the Ragged School Union, in 1844, with many Ragged Schools being established for thousands of poor children. But the growth of more widespread education, particularly for girls, was hindered because teachers themselves were often uneducated. Many unmarried women drifted into teaching as an alternative to domestic work or to becoming a companion. Even so, the advance of increasing education continued.

During the 1840s, as the techniques and speed of printing progressed, spelling books, primers and readers, grammars, catechisms, pocket histories, 'geographies' and introductions to mathematics and natural history were produced in comparatively large quantities. More publishers started issuing reading books, although they were mostly stilted and not graded according to the ability of barely literate children. Many books were in question and answer form, while others had long pieces on inappropriate subjects. A passage proposing fresh air at night, called On Sleeping Comfortably, contended that:

> 'As boiling water does not grow hotter by longer boiling, if the particles that receive greater heat can escape, so living bodies do not putrify if the particles, as fast as they become putrid, can be thrown off.'

This was from *The Juvenile Reader* and approved by the Committee of Council for Education, whose secretary, by contrast, compiled *The First Phonic Reading Book.*

In 1844 the SPCK was selling a well-bound new testament for sixpence, but their 'Education Series' called *First Reading Book* cost one shilling and sixpence for each part. New books were increasingly needed, as the number of children at St Martin's grew, but rules of the SPCK meant there could be no discount on secular books. So the bible and *Exposition of the Church Catechism* continued being used as 'readers', until more suitable books were widely available and the price had been reduced.

Money was not as forthcoming as it had been in earlier days, and in 1847 the vicar of St Martin-in-the-Fields, the Reverend Sir Henry Dunkinfield, sent out a long letter to his parishioners stating the need for an extra annual subscription to help maintain parochial charities. These included the several schools in the five ecclesiastical districts. In his letter giving his reasons, he wrote:

> 'The Masters and Mistresses of our schools are entitled to very great commendation for the order and proficiency to which the schools have been brought.' And he added: 'A great many of the principal houses which were recently inhabited by wealthy families, who contributed largely to the support of our charities, are now engaged for government or other offices and our sources of income are thus materially diminished.'

Despite this lack of money, new clothes continued to be bought each year. And each year the children joined the procession for the charity schools and other public occasions, when they walked two by two in their long line through the streets to church. By now walking had become a regular daily exercise, too, even though it was reported that:

> 'Frequent walks rather interfere with the quantity of the work done in the School, and cause the shoes and stockings to wear out faster.'

Fortunately, a rider was added that the walks were 'very advantageous to the health of the children'. But daily exercise also caused more wear to their outdoor clothes particularly as 'the straw bonnets are less solid than they used to be'. So straw bonnets, 'prepared as usual for Ascension Day', had to be replaced each year.

Health problems continued to dog the dedicated schoolmistresses, and in September 1848 Mrs McCleary was allowed a short absence 'for the benefit of Country air and repose which is necessary for her health'. But once again the holiday appears to have been too late and a successor, Mrs Terry, took over from the hard worked Mrs McCleary. In September 1850 the Ladies' Committee recorded:

> 'The Visiting Lady has found the School in good order & the Children healthy, and she trusts the well-being of the establishment will be preserved as prosperously under the new management as it was for so many years under the faithful and judicious care of its late Matron, Mrs McClary, who for a long period gave great satisfaction to the successive vicars and to the Committee of Ladies who were always unanimous in bearing testimony to her exemplary good conduct, and to the efficient manner in which she discharged the duties of her situation.'

Under Mrs Terry's administration the girls' bright yellow mittens were finally replaced with mittens to match their dresses. Like the ribbons earlier, they looked too conspicuous, and now the need to be seen as a charity school was not so necessary.

There was great excitement on the day of the Prince of Wales' marriage, as the school lined the streets to see the procession and glimpse Princess Alexandra of Denmark, the Princess of Wales. Afterwards the children were given a special tea to mark the happy occasion. Earlier, a wry comment had been made that with the Prince of Wales now an inhabitant of the parish, 'funds will not be wanting to maintain the school in its efficiency'.

When a new menu was devised for Sunday breakfast, beer was no longer included. Instead bread and milk and water were provided each morning, and bread and butter with milk and water each evening. At the same time the midday meal became more varied with one pint of barley broth or 'pease' soup, or meat pies as alternatives to boiled or roast mutton or beef. Vegetables in season were served once or twice a week and potatoes on every meat day. But there were still three days with just rice pudding, suet pudding or 'plumb' pudding.

Beyond the school, with its problems of coloured mittens and new bonnets, the Industrial Revolution was making even greater demands for more widespread education, as the nation could no longer cope with the 'large burden of ignorance'. Yet it was not until 1862 that the Committee of Council for Education had stipulated definite reading standards at different levels for younger children, even though Oxford and Cambridge local examinations for boys had been introduced four years earlier.

At that time, women were thought to be 'freakish' if they had been able to take advantage of a broader education than normal — either by being self-taught through copious reading, or because of enlightened parents providing teachers and access to knowledge. And there were still many who felt there was a physical difference in the structure of the female brain, which made women unalterably inferior to men. However, the pioneers gradually proved that education was not only possible but enjoyable, so the old belief started to decline as education for girls and young women began to be seen as a necessity.

When W.E. Forster introduced the Elementary Education Act of 1870 he said:

> 'On the speedy provision of elementary education depends our industrial prosperity.'

Education to enhance people as *people* was not yet envisaged, but the Act was a great leap forward.

Under the Act, where no voluntary school existed, public elementary education was to be provided, under the authority of local school boards. 'Board Schools' would be set up alongside national schools, to give more co-ordinated provision throughout the country. For fives to tens education would soon be compulsory, and a certificate of proficiency and minimum attendance would be necessary if ten to fourteen year olds were employed.

To avoid the old inter-denominational wrangles, board schools were to be non-sectarian. And there was to be a 'conscience clause' to enable parents to withdraw their children from religious instruction, both in board and voluntary government-aided schools. Teachers in board schools were to be certificated, and the schools open to inspection at all times, with annual examinations to determine the amount of grant. The basic reading standards, introduced eight years earlier, were also revised:

Standard	
I	One of the narratives next in order after monosyllables in an elementary reading book used in the school.
II	A short paragraph from an elementary reading book.
III	A short paragraph from a more advanced reading book.
IV	A few lines of poetry or prose.
V	A short ordinary paragraph in a newspaper, or modern narrative.
VI	To read with fluency and expression.

But just as this first education act was being debated in parliament, St Martin's trustees were debating the future of their own school. For rather than being absorbed into the board school system, or being taken over by the National Society like many other charity schools, the trustees decided on a complete change of direction. This became possible after 1869 when the Endowed Schools Act was passed, marking a significant change in education for girls.

The change was partly due to the persistence of Emily Davies, one of the pioneers in education for women who pleaded on behalf of girls' education. This prompted the school commissioners to examine the few secondary schools that were available for girls. The contrast between their visits to girls' schools struggling to keep going, and their visit to Cheltenham Ladies' College emphasised the opportunities that could be available for girls when the right backing was provided. Their visit finally convinced the commissioners that funds allocated to endowed schools for boys should be shared equally with girls' schools.

For St Martin's to take advantage of this latest development, radical changes would have to be made. A new, much larger building would be needed, and planning began to set the school on an exciting new footing.

2. Charing Cross Days: 1870 - 1928

Moving to the purpose-built, four storey school at 15 Charing Cross
Road marked a new direction for St Martin's. Plans had been drawn
up by the architect, Arthur Blomfield, to include a large 'drill room',
six class rooms, a small 'receiving room', an apartment for the
headmistress and a cloakroom in the basement. Vaults under the
small playground were also to be constructed.

The cost was not to exceed £3,500, which would include furnishings, fittings, design and architect's fees, together with 'hot water
apparatus and gas fittings'. The front of the building would be dominated by large windows, each one divided into small panes, with two
dormer windows in the roof. There were to be steps leading up to the
massive front door and more steps going down to the basement. At
first the name 'St Martin's Endowed Middle School for Girls' was
used. Later it would change to the full St Martin-in-the-Fields High
School for Girls.

With 150 girls from seven years upwards, several schoolmistresses would now be needed. Fortunately, women's colleges were gradually being created, and a trickle of trained teachers was beginning to
appear. Various individual associations had been promoting
women's education and training, and this fragmented interest came
together in 1871 as the 'National Union for improving the education
of women of all classes'.

Although public schools and endowed grammar schools for boys
continued to flourish, secondary education for girls was now easier
to set up. Other charity schools changed their status, including
Christ's Hospital, Red Maids' School at Bristol, and the Grey Coat
Hospital which separated into two endowed schools, one for boys,
the other for girls.

St Martin's old building, in Heming's Row, was sold to the

Commissioners of Woods and Forests under the National Gallery Enlargement Act. Much later, in 1896, a new building would be built for the National Portrait Gallery, and later still groups of St Martin's girls would visit the Gallery with Miss Thomas, as part of their history lessons.

By September 1874 St Martin's new building was completed and ready to receive fifty Swedish desks, which were added to from time to time. The following year iron gates at the entrance to the school would 'protect the steps', and a board bearing the school name would

St Martin's in Charing Cross Road
(School archives)

be set in place. But to start with there were many problems to overcome.

To set the school off in its new quarters, the board of governors, headed by the vicar of St Martin-in-the-Fields, the Revd. William Humphry, appointed Miss C.C. Derrick as the new headmistress.

Miss Derrick had been Assistant Mistress at the North London Collegiate College, where she was greatly influenced by Miss Frances Mary Buss. Francis Mary Buss had founded the college after attending part-time training from the newly-opened Queen's College, a foundation of the Governesses Benevolent Institution. And from the age of fourteen, she had gained much practical experience as a pupil-teacher before starting her first school when she was eighteen.

The Collegiate College, founded four years later, was way ahead of its time with a curriculum that included English, scripture, history, geography, arithmetic, French, elementary Latin, drawing, singing and callisthenics (exercises for health and beauty). Italian, German, music, painting and dancing were also offered as extra subjects, and some subjects were taught by lecturers from Queen's College, which itself covered an even more ambitious curriculum.

There is no record that St Martin's followed such a full syllabus, but with this background Miss Derrick would have had high aims for her school. Miss Derrick was also one of the nine pioneers who founded the Association of Head Mistresses, in 1874, under the leadership of Frances Mary Buss. The purpose of the association was to overcome the many problems envisaged for girls' secondary education. With Miss Derrick as a founder member, St Martin's would inevitably benefit from its progressive thinking.

Many questions needed to be answered, and Dr Edward Thring, headmaster of Uppingham, was later to say:

> 'You are fresh and enthusiastic and completely untrammelled whilst we are weighed down by tradition, cast like iron in the rigid moulds of the past. . .'

The pattern of the school year changed, with termly examinations instead of quarterly as in earlier years. And holidays meant a schoolmistress no longer had to ask for a short absence 'for the benefit of Country air and repose which is necessary for her health'. But although boys had Saturday morning lessons, these were not considered suitable for girls, as a conference report for the Association of Head Mistresses stated:

> '. . . there must be no suggestion that the girls were being prevented from helping their mothers in week-end shopping and other domestic tasks.'

Girls' endowed secondary schools may have been breaking new ground, but from the start, prejudices still had to be overcome and changing views gradually accepted.

Miss Derrick stayed at St Martin's for ten years, and an Old Girl was later to describe her as 'a grave little lady, her hair dressed high in little ringlets'. By another Old Girl she was remembered for her:

> 'Dancing ringlets, as grey as her frock; standing at the head of the stairs and rapping a pencil on the rail as we filed down in step from the classroom to the "Drill Room" for morning prayers, where we stood in serried rows'.

37

Sadly, Miss Derrick, like so many of her predecessors, retired due to ill-health and died only six months later. But she had set the school on its new path, with a high standard of efficiency.

Miss Mary Pullée was the next headmistress to be appointed, and accounts of her say she was 'progressive and not content with mediocrity'. Her sympathy with schoolgirl difficulties, her bracing words of encouragement, or at times reproof, marked her strong personality. Her habit of swaying 'a tip-toe' as she spoke, 'as if poised for some great endeavour', was also remembered. And it was said that 'into all her work was infused that living spark which revealed the personality behind the teacher'.

Hester Williams (later to become Principal of the Diocesan Training College, Derby) recalled her school days at Charing Cross when she wrote:

> 'We must have found it very difficult to be punctual for morning school, for I vividly remember our scampers along Heming's Row, and our relief on turning into Castle Street, if we could see "the gate monitor" looking this way and that in search of laggards before she slammed the heavy iron gate into the basement entry. Morning assembly we always felt to be a special feature of the school day. The chapter chosen for repetition was memorised, verse by verse, along the row of children until the whole was achieved — and long remembered. A hymn followed, and then Miss Pullée had generally something to say which brought our thoughts and interests together before we separated for classes.'

Having left the drill room/dining room/hall there was a strict rule of no talking. A large hand bell stood on the first landing, and this was rung by a prefect to summon girls to lessons. Some girls 'forgot' their duty at the end of a lesson, if it was one they particularly liked.

Girls who misbehaved in class were sent outside the room. They first had to tick off their names on a list hanging by the door, but sometimes a girl ticked over an existing tick if she thought no one would notice. The miscreant then waited on the landing until she felt repentant enough to ask to rejoin the class. Occasionally she would hear Miss Pullée cough before she started up the stairs to the landing. Some girls believed the 'cough' was a deliberate warning, so they could scuttle back to their classroom before Miss Pullée appeared.

The wide sweep of the new Charing Cross Road brought the school to the fore, but it also brought more noisy traffic. So, too, did the building of the new Vestry Hall (Westminster City Hall), which was completed in 1891 and opened by the Prince of Wales. But the new hall provided a spacious setting for school prize giving, instead of the cramped conditions of the rather drab drill room. On these occasions the whole school walked in a dignified 'crocodile' along the streets to the hall. The Duchess of York or the Duchess of Teck, accompanied by Princess May, sometimes distributed the prizes of beautiful leather-bound books.

In the same way that the charity children had lined the streets to watch royal processions, these later girls of St Martin's watched too, but this time sitting on special seats erected in the portico of St Martin's Church. And this time there were no bright yellow mittens and ribbons to show their status, just the neat navy blue school uniform, with velour hats in winter and cream boaters in summertime — and no girl would ever be seen without her gloves.

The girls were not always ladylike. One morning Winnie Fitzgerald cycled to school trying to see how far she could cycle with her eyes closed! But a lamp post in Leicester Square and concussion quickly ended her cycle ride. Fortunately it was a lamp post and not a moving vehicle, for the mixture of horse drawn and mechanised traffic was increasing.

Added to the noise were the sounds of St Martin's church bells ringing out for weddings, funerals and services, or just being practised. In hot weather, if the school windows were open the noise of London streets filled the rooms, while from the back came sounds of boys from Archbishop Tenison's School drilling to music beyond the high brick wall that separated the two playgrounds. But if the windows were kept shut it became stiflingly hot in the classrooms.

As St Martin's neared its bicentenary, the Royal Commission on Education made several changes to the code of practice. One of these was to abolish grants paid to schools by crude results, in favour of more flexibility. The highest awards were given for reading and reciting from memory. A further grant was given to girls for successful passes in cookery and laundry work, while drawing for boys and needlework for girls were obligatory. The general report for 1891 given by the senior chief inspector, Reverend T.W. Sharpe, stated:

> 'Beyond reading, writing, arithmetic, drawing, singing and needlework, no scholar, as a rule, learns more than two class subjects (geography, grammar, history and elementary science). In addition to this in some of the best schools the older boys and girls are entitled to study one or two of the long list of specific subjects enumerated in the Code; mechanics for boys and domestic economy for girls are the favourite subjects in London.'

Two years later, the school leaving age was raised to eleven, and to twelve in 1899, even though it was still legal to employ children in factories from the age of eleven.

In 1897 a small five-year-old called Lydia Mentasti, wearing a stiff straw boater and brown overcoat over her full, dark blue skirt and woollen top, walked to school accompanied by her maid. Seventy-five years later, Lydia talked of her life at St Martin's:

> 'School began at nine o'clock and ended at four o'clock. Short boots were worn to travel to and from school, but once at school they would be changed for house shoes. Nobody rebelled against her hat because it was just not done to go out without one. Gloves were worn as a matter of course for every journey no matter how small. The one break in the day was from half past twelve until two o'clock. There was no mid-morning break. School lunch was not provided but everybody took sandwiches, and milk could be ordered through the school.
>
> 'In French lessons nothing was learnt about France, and only English history was studied. Latin or German could be learnt but not both. There were art lessons in which the girls drew flowers and painted still life, but there was no craft or pottery. In cookery and dressmaking girls could ask questions about their work, but general conversation was forbidden. A master visited the school to teach songs which were mainly cantatas. The only other music lessons were those on the piano or, if very lucky, the violin.
>
> 'Girls were chaperoned to Archbishop Tenison Boys' School for chemistry. There were usually no boys about, but it would have been against the rules to speak to them if there were. No practical science with apparatus was

done at all, and there was no physics, so girls spent a lot of time doing botany, dissecting flowers.

'School exams mainly decided whether girls graduated to the next class. Age made no difference in classes as girls were grouped according to ability. Everybody had to provide her own blotting paper, pencils, text books, and girls always stood up to answer a question; they took this for granted. Fees were about three guineas per term, except for a very small percentage of scholarship girls.

'Discipline was quite strict. On pulling a face at the thought of the next lesson a girl was sent to the headmistress. Detention with one hundred lines was often the form of punishment given to those who misbehaved. There were monitors but they spent most of their time looking after the plants in the classrooms!'

By 1902 School Boards were abolished, when board schools were brought under county and county boroughs' control through Local Education Authorities (LEAs), with further powers to provide secondary education. The need for more secondary education and the increase in population both affected St Martin's, so numbers grew.

The problem of city noise had also increased, and this prompted the London County Council (LCC) to suggest that St Martin's should be moved out to the suburbs, 'where pupils would abound and the school would have a prosperous future'. Education inspectors also urged the school to be moved, and in 1905 they referred to:

'. . .the unsuitability of the present site and the difficulty or impossibility of obtaining a better one in the same district. . .[And] owing to the migration of the residential population from the central districts, the existing provision is inadequate.'

Even so, numbers had increased to 180, and space for gymnastics and sports was a particular problem.

One year a Drill Display, with pupils wearing thick pleated tunics and black woollen stockings, was held in the crypt of St Martin's Church so that parents and visitors could watch. The vicar of St Martin's, the Reverend Dick Sheppard, also allowed the school to use St Martin's Hall, where multi-national dancing displays and rhythmic gymnastics with wands, sashes and dumb-bells became popular events.

41

On a few memorable occasions hockey matches took place on Clapham Common, and in the summer, cricket was held in Regent's Park. But visiting schools arriving for netball matches would complain about the under-sized netball court. Later, when St Martin's played an away match, with Marylebone High School, they were quite unused to the full-sized court.

After cookery lessons in the dimly-lit basement, girls trailed up through the school to the housekeeper's flat on the top floor, where Mrs Burchell would pop the dishes into her own gleaming range. But this inconvenience was offset on cold winter days when Mrs Burchell, 'a jolly, buxom and motherly soul', would give the girls warm milk to drink while they sat round her cosy fire.

Following much discussion, the majority of governors gradually agreed that a move out of London was necessary, due to the increased noise in Charing Cross which 'renders the work of the Mistresses not only painfully laborious but also injurious to them'. And so the long search began, to find a new site for St Martin's. But in the meantime school in the noisy classrooms continued.

In describing her 'happy times at St Martin's', Ruby Farrow remembered 'Cambridge Week', when the botany exam was taken in the evening, and concentration was interrupted by sounds of a barrel-organ being played to queues outside the Garrick Theatre opposite the school. She remembered having a holiday on the centenary of Nelson's death because of the crowds in Trafalgar Square. She saw the first coloured educational films, and 'motor-buses towed by triumphant cart-horses'. Then came the 'new' Latin pronunciation and 'lovely Friday afternoons devoted to art'. At a time when aeroplanes were a novelty, another of her memories was:

'. . . making people in Charing Cross Road look up at a non-existent aeroplane. We used to crowd to the window if we ever had the chance and look up into the air.'

Lack of space in the drill room, where younger girls ate their sandwiches, gave older girls the privilege of going out of school for their lunch. Sixth-formers were also allowed to eat their sandwiches as they huddled round the small gas fire in the sixth form room. Prefects had other privileges, too, one of which was entering the school by going *up* the steps to ring the front door bell, while the orderly line of smaller girls, waiting patiently by the school railings, went *down* the steps to the basement cloakroom.

London's Underground brought more people into the City with noise and bustle increasing. Yet the opportunity to visit museums, art galleries, exhibitions, theatres and to attend lectures was always there and often taken.

It wasn't until 1908 that Silwood House, on the top of Tulse Hill in South London, was found and thought suitable as a new home for the school. Prolonged negotiations were nearing completion by the summer of 1912 when, after twenty-seven years' service at St Martin's, Miss Pullée retired, although she remained in constant touch with all the school's activities.

Miss Clare Bannister, her successor, continued the negotiations which were finally completed in 1913. Plans were prepared for the new building and tenders invited, but all had to be shelved when war broke out in 1914. Fathers, brothers, cousins, uncles left home to join the countless number of servicemen abroad. Many did not return.

At school, lessons were interrupted by air raids, and partial rationing was introduced. Huge silver zeppelins were seen flying slowly across the sky, and 'hostile machines' on moonlit raids dropped bombs on London. The school continued unharmed throughout the war, although many years later Miss Bannister was to refer to the school's 'trying experiences' and of the 'courage shown by both the members of the staff and the girls'.

Remembering the war years, Maude Bacon (née Hayward) said:

> 'We knitted gloves and balaclava helmets for the troops, sang patriotic songs and staged appropriate plays, but not until the zeppelins came over did it really touch me. Full realization came when my only brother was killed in France in 1916.'

After this event, Miss Bannister's kindness was never forgotten, because she arranged for Maude to have a holiday with her friends in the country.

Long after the war, Phyllis Baxter (née Cooper) was to write:

> 'St Martin's in the days of the first World War. What myriad small memories come crowding to my mind! The chatter in the basement cloakroom, stilled by an occasional voice of authority, "Less noise, girls, please." The washing-up of dinner mugs and plates in the same cloakroom (leaving them to *drain* on Fridays!). Sitting in the basement during air raids.
>
> 'The tiny playground; the netball matches; strolling round at lunch time or break, arm-in-arm with one's special crony. Ringing the front door-bell the first time I was late; being kept in on Friday afternoon with the rest of Form Va, after unruly conduct at netball, and under Miss Dunnicliff's eye paraphrasing *Gray's Elegy*, with surreptitious glances at Tennyson's playground! The big bell on the landing; the hum and sudden hush in the hall at Prayers; the neat files and "block" paper; the pride of a "Best" with "C.H.B." in red; the thrill of receiving a Leader's Badge; waiting at Leicester Square station to carry a mistress's case. Memories of St Martin's! Memories of a happy, homely school.'

And the 'happy, homely school' joined in the celebrations as soon as the war had ended.

On Armistice Day London was packed with cheering crowds thronging the streets. There was no holiday from school, and Brenda Field (née Reeve) recalled that her class crowded to the window with their tall, slim, French mistress, Mlle Dehors de St Mondé, 'a never to be forgotten lady'. Mademoiselle, who wore unusually heavy make-up, was often so emotional that tears would stream down her face taking her make-up with them. But on this particular day she became so excited she was in danger of falling from the window, as she leant out shouting:

> 'Fillettes, la guerre est finie! Vive la France! Et l'Angleterre!'

A combined United Thanksgiving Service was held at St Martin-in-the-Fields Church in July 1919, when girls from Grey Coat Hospital, Francis Holland School and Burlington School joined the girls of St Martin's. As they filed quietly into the church the sounds of Handel's *Largo*, played by HM Band of the Welsh Guards, rang through the ancient building. Thereafter, on Armistice Day, silence was observed at 11 o'clock on the eleventh day of the eleventh month each year, when all the traffic and bustle of the City stopped for two minutes. On these occasions the sounds of Big Ben and St Martin-in-the-Fields' clock could clearly be heard.

With the war over, the Ministry of Health was created, and a new Education Act was also passed. This time the school leaving age was raised to fourteen, and no child of school age could be employed in a mine or factory. The half-time system of education and industry was ended, the employment of children under twelve was abolished and children between twelve and fourteen could only work for two hours. Although many other proposed schemes were not implemented, the Act revealed the change in attitude that education for children was more important than child labour.

In 1919 plans for the school at Tulse Hill were drawn up once more, but again all had to be abandoned, this time because of the need for national economy which caused Lord Geddes to propose cuts in public health and education, for by now the post-war slump was starting.

Four school Houses were set up now that the school was to continue at Charing Cross. And soon friendly rivalry took place between St Martin's (House), St George's, St Andrew's and St Patrick's. Two years later a fifth House, St Francis, was made up from members of the four existing Houses. A House flag was presented to the school by the chairman of the governors, Mr Dudley James, and each year there was keen competition to 'own' it for the following year.

The House system worked well, with around thirty girls of mixed ages in each. Prefects and older girls helped and encouraged the 'little people', spurring them on to greater heights. Each girl felt part of the team with a pride in her achievement, whether working in lessons or at games to get House points or in trying not to 'let down the side'. There were picnics and parties, as well as concerts and fund-raising events too.

From the proceeds of a concert, St Patrick's House bought a 'Union Jack' and presented it to the school. When the flag was given to Miss Bannister one morning after prayers, Ruby Bryant 'held it to the salute while the National Anthem was sung'.

Until 1922 magazines were produced by the Houses, then House news was incorporated into a school magazine with all the varied activities of the whole school. The first issue proudly gave the previous year's examination successes for Cambridge Senior Local Examinations. It was possible to take these in July 1921, but only a few years before the school had moved to Charing Cross, heated debates took place to decide whether girls should be allowed to take university local, and ultimately university entrance, examinations. London and Oxford Universities had rejected the idea, suggesting separate exams for girls, to prevent competition with boys.

However, once again due to the persistence of Emily Davies, the intrepid educationalist who had pushed for endowment grants for girls' schools, Cambridge University had finally agreed that girls could take Cambridge local examinations identical to those taken by boys. Emily Davies had hurriedly rounded up eighty-three girls to sit for the senior and junior exams. And despite gloomy predictions that the girls would collapse from 'nervous hysteria' and later 'die of brain-fever', the girls remained unscathed. Such satisfactory results were achieved (apart from arithmetic for both boys and girls) that all argument dissolved and from that time Cambridge local examinations became possible for girls.

But higher education was still regarded as unsuitable for young women in those days, and it was a few more years before the Cambridge Women's Examinations, as a means of entry to women's colleges at the University, provided an increasing number of girls this opportunity.

Once examinations were well established, more girls stayed on at St Martin's and more began to stay after taking Cambridge locals. The sixth form enlarged to twelve girls and for several years the numbers stayed constant. By 1922 General School Certificate (GSC) examinations and Matriculation were introduced. For St Martin's girls these exams were taken at Hampstead Town Hall. Roxanne Arnold went on to take a degree in economics, and later followed with a degree in law. Later still, she was to become a barrister, at a time when few women practised law.

It may have been because of the school's early foundation as a charity school, and subsequent years of accepting the generosity of many people, that St Martin's has always collected for charity. Like many other schools, collecting week by week, class by class, became part of school life.

When the Reigate Orphans Home had closed, the school's Orphan Fund subscription was transferred to Great Ormond Street Hospital for Sick Children. Thereafter, regular termly or annual contributions were collected from staff, Old Girls and girls alike, whose contributions ranged from three shillings to threepence halfpenny. A 'farthing fund', started by St Patrick's House, with 'generous contributions from the kindergarten and transition', was added to money from the sale of unclaimed lost property and amounted to nearly £18. Donations to the General Hospital Fund were also made by many London schools, with a target of £5,000 by Christmas 1922.

Another charity that was supported by St Martin's, year after year, was the Ranyard Mission. A magazine report for 1922 began:

'During the Autumn Term of each year the School is very busy making children's garments of all kinds to help to stock the cupboards of the Ranyard Mission in Russell Square. Their nurses — who do district work in a great many poor parishes in London — are always glad to have our large bundles of clothing to distribute. . .'

Money and contributions of tea, sugar, tapioca, cornflour and jam were also sent, and toys were collected for the children each Christmas. Although sewing the garments was incorporated into needlework lessons, any money-raising events for charities were normally carried on after school as another magazine report confirmed:

'In response to a special appeal last Summer, we sent a donation of £2.10s to the Children's Country Holiday Fund. The money was largely raised by impromptu efforts in the different Forms, such as a Jumble Sale, a Sale of Fruit and Flowers, and an impromptu Concert, all taking place for about half an hour at the end of afternoon School.'

These simple efforts seemed to set a pattern of concern from which hospitals, disaster funds and many charities benefited.

Through all this activity the site at Tulse Hill was not forgotten. In the summer term of 1923 each class made weekly excursions there, travelling on the top deck of a number thirty-three tram to use the spacious grounds for games, sports and nature study. Giving details of the scheme for using the grounds, Miss Bannister wrote:

> 'Tennis nets and net-ball apparatus were purchased, school gardens prepared for use, outdoor lessons arranged in Botany, English, Practical Mathematics etc.; indoor shelter was provided, and a gramophone purchased for use at Country Dancing classes.'

Eventually, Miss Bannister agreed that hockey could also be played, although she thought hockey was decidedly unladylike.

Lessons in the fresh air, sitting under the sweeping branches of a cedar tree, were a delight. When it rained the girls hurried into Silwood House, now in a sorry state of disrepair, to continue their lessons or eat their midday sandwiches sitting on the floor of the garden room. And soon another highlight of the year for each House became their annual picnic at Tulse Hill.

Although most activities were centred around the Houses, there was one competition to gain points that was inter-form. This was in two sections for each of the sets of classrooms on the upper and lower landings:

> 1.) For beauty and order of the rooms
> 2.) For excellent order of lines on the stairs.

The comment was added that this was 'always a difficulty in our narrow building'. Each term keen rivalry developed among the forms, and not only were the classrooms kept tidy and neat, but flowers often adorned them. The winning classes in each section won a class picture to hang in their room for the following term. If one class won a section for three consecutive terms, the picture became the permanent possession of the class.

In 1924 a fund was set up in memory of Miss Allen who had taught at St Martin's from 1880 to 1915, and who had died in

December 1923. The fund, called the Allan Loan Memorial, was to enable 'girls who having obtained their first certificate would be unable to continue their studies'. As a loan fund the money would later be returned so that other girls could benefit. Money was initially raised by selling war savings certificates, and through concerts, sales and donations, contributions continued for many years.

The need to help increased as the slump in the twenties became deeper. In 1926, with the added hardship of the general strike, many people, young and old, became dependent on charity. One headmistress asked St Martin's for outgrown gym slips and shoes so that girls going to the sea for a holiday would be 'suitably clad'.

The general strike also caused travel chaos, and getting to work or school became a test of ingenuity. Gwen Creek (née Botten) recalled:

> 'On one occasion I rode in a yellow four-horse brake with all its trappings and jingling harness, which attracted great attention as we clattered along the Euston Road. Soon a lorry service was started from Trafalgar Square for North London and it became the regular mode of transport for St Martin's girls for a few days. We mounted the lorry by a ladder and stood huddled together for the whole of the journey, the driver avoiding the main roads because gangs of strikers on the street corners were ready to cause trouble. One of these lorries must have come straight from Covent Garden, because one day, to everybody's amusement, we drove through the London streets labelled "Choice Peaches".'

Going home from school on the first day of the strike fifth-former Mary Tout managed to catch a private bus. Later she wrote:

> 'At Camden Town we were met by an angry crowd of strikers, who attempted to stop the bus, but they were soon dispersed by mounted police. On one bus, which was being driven by a volunteer, I saw written "A rolling bus gathers no stones". On another — "A brick in the hand is worth two in the bus", while another rather dilapidated looking bus had written on it "Please don't stop us, as we took three hours to start". Another bus that had nearly all its windows broken, bore the words, "Painless extractions".'

The good-humour of volunteers and cheerful willingness to help thus alleviated some of the hardship of travel. Tube trains, one of which was painted with teddy bears, were driven by undergraduates;

pantechnicons were pulled into service; and one girl travelled to school in a greengrocer's cart drawn by a donkey.

Another fifth-former, Marie Curtis, showed great stamina when she set off at 7 o'clock in the morning from Kenton. She and her sister, who was going to work, had planned to walk, and not knowing the route decided they could follow the tramlines once they reached Wembley. But 'on arriving at Wembley we saw on a sign post "London 8 miles".' Undaunted they carried on walking, reaching Willesden by 8 o'clock where:

> 'Everyone was stirring; shopkeepers were taking down their shutters and arranging their goods . . . housewives were making their doors and windows bright and clean.'

Cars, grocery vans, motorcycles, 'ordinary carts' and bicycles passed them along the roads, 'every conveyance full to overflowing, but everyone was cheerful.'

An hour later the intrepid walkers had reached Kilburn, where 'groups of men were talking moodily together.' A few more sign posts further on the sisters parted. Marie walked the last two miles to Charing Cross, arriving at school by 10 o'clock — a feat of great endurance which few schoolchildren would undertake, but one which must have caused the sisters immense satisfaction. Fortunately the strike ended nine days later and travelling to school was back to normal.

Immense satisfaction resulted on sports days, too, when with great excitement the whole school transferred to Tulse Hill from Charing Cross. Many parents, friends and governors also made the trek, to line the field and cheer the fleeting, flying, running girls.

At first, sports days were held in the afternoon only, then, as the number of races increased, heats were held in the morning and finals in the afternoon. Serious sports were simple 'flat races', but fun sports included obstacle, sack, three-legged and thread the needle races. Later came a potato race. House flag races were also held, and when senior and junior high jump competitions were included the winning jump in each section was 4ft 2ins. But 1926 was to be the last sports day after travelling down from Charing Cross, as work on the new school building at Tulse Hill had begun.

After many negotiations and amendments it had been decided that Silwood House should be incorporated into the design, so that the impressive front would give an imposing entrance to the school. The large, lofty rooms would be used for staff rooms, secretary's office, library, music room, sick room and a flat for the caretakers.

The whole of the back of the house would be taken down enabling a long, four-storey extension to be butted on. It would cover much of the garden but leave the field beyond intact for sports and games as before. Optimistically there was talk of the building being finished by the autumn of 1927, and older girls hoped they might still be at school to appreciate all the new building would offer.

In the meantime there were still the benefits of city life. Art was appreciated by sixth-formers on Wednesday mornings, when they arrived at the National Gallery just as it opened. Under the guidance of Miss Edith Neville, a friend of Miss Bannister, they studied the different schools of art, amply depicted by the exhibits. Gwen Creek remembered thinking the freshly polished floors were so shiny 'it was a pity to walk on them'. Afterwards, the smell of fresh floor polish always reminded her of those 'delightful Wednesday mornings'. Other visits, though necessitating longer journeys, included the Wallace Collection and the Tate Gallery.

Walking in a neatly dressed crocodile through the subway to the Science and Natural History Museums was another bonus of school in the City. A further bonus came the day Miss Thomas rounded up her senior history class and walked them along Whitehall to watch the pageantry of the opening of parliament. For older girls, many hours were spent in the poetry bookshop, in Holborn, listening to John Masefield, John Drinkwater and Walter de la Mare reading their poems. Here were history, art, poetry and music all within reach of St Martin's.

A room had been set aside for music in the school basement, a small room with a large piano which, in a description by Marie Curtis, 'seemed to elongate itself into a table, so close the two had to be'. Once fire drill was established, the music room acted as a fire exit out to the playground. On these infrequent occasions, the connecting door was unlocked in the high wall through to the boys' school. But as this congested exit was seen as a potential death-trap, the main entrance was later used to evacuate the school for fire drill, and the music room no longer had this potentially dangerous use.

In the early 1920s, examinations in 'pianoforte and rudiments of music' were taken for the Associated Board of the Royal Academy of Music and the Royal College of Music. By 1926 the exams had divided into primary, elementary, lower, higher and advanced levels, with girls gaining certificates in each section.

With this interest in music, concerts were organised through the Houses, often to raise money for a particular charity. The idea of charity concerts may have been prompted when fifth-formers visited Wigmore Hall to hear a concert in aid of the Ranyard Mission. Once back at school, songs and piano pieces were practised and performed with great enthusiasm.

On another occasion it was the fourth forms' turn to be involved with an outside concert. Community singing, arranged by the *Daily Express*, was held at Central Hall Westminster, with not just singing but solos and orchestral pieces under the baton of Dr Malcolm Sargent. Visits to Covent Garden Theatre were arranged, too, and one afternoon a large party of girls went to *The Magic Flute* performed by the British Opera Company.

Being so close to the hub of things, there were many other outings to enjoy, with visits to the Imperial Institute, St Katharine's Docks, Australia House, the Botanical Gardens, Houses of Parliament, St Paul's and Westminster Abbey. Travelling around London had been made easier when the Underground had been extended, and Eileen State recalled memories of:

'Travelling by Tube, often on the open platform with the guard, to a clanging accompaniment from iron gates at every station; scrambling up the emergency stairs to avoid the newly-installed escalator; or a journey on the top of a bumpy open 'bus, mackintosh apron over knees, or if need be on my head. If the fog came down, yellow and soupy, or if a procession such as the Lord Mayor's threatened to complicate travelling, we went home early.'

The British Empire Exhibition caused much interest, when almost the whole school set off in four private buses for Wembley. The Palace of Industry intrigued the girls with its manufacturing processes and machinery from many Empire countries. They were especially delighted by the South African train, the fascinating street of shops from Hong Kong and an orchard of Canadian apple trees hanging with fruit. Marjorie Winter-Moy, a fourth-former, summed up her visit when she said:

'We had learnt in that one day at Wembley more than we could have learnt in a whole year of study.'

Yet, school provided a wealth of interest through visiting lecturers talking on subjects as diverse as Egypt, Ruskin and Jane Austen.

After hearing a talk about the League of Nations the school set up its own junior branch, to give talks on first-hand information about the League's work. Miss Bannister and six older girls went to a lecture at Kingsway Hall given by Lord Robert Cecil, Britain's League of Nations representative. And St Martin's staff and sixth form acted as stewards at a 3,000 strong rally at Central Hall, Westminster. The following year a fifth-former visited the headquarters in Geneva, as the school's representative.

In 1927 young people from all over the world took part in a Festival of Youth, held at Crystal Palace. St Martin's was well represented, entering dolls dressed in various national costumes and by coming fifth in the essay competition. There were stalls to visit, athletic competitions and folk dancing displays arranged by different countries. In this way, the League of Nations tried to ensure worldwide peace by encouraging youth involvement.

In school or out of school, standards of work and behaviour were rigorously maintained. Miss Bannister was said to glide about gracefully, never raising her voice, but 'you could have heard a pin drop when she entered a classroom'. Connie Clarke (née Sargent) remembered one occasion when the pin was dropped. Mlle Dehors de St Mondé, in her lively exuberance, had taught her French class to sing *Ma Normandie*. To add to the effect, girls were allowed to accompany the boisterous singing on a 'comb band' (comb and paper). In full crescendo, the door opened, in walked a severe Miss Bannister and the singing abruptly stopped.

In maths, girls wrote out theorems on miniature blackboards, and sometimes 'May-Go-Down' would be written on good work. This meant girls could carry their work with pride down the stairs to Miss Bannister's office for her approval. And good or bad, work would be registered on the termly report card.

For bad behaviour girls were still sent outside the room, where they stood 'on the mat' hoping Miss Bannister wouldn't see them.

'Her cold disapproval would shrivel the stoutest heart,' commented Maude Bacon, 'every action, every emotion "tailored" to the last degree. . .Not till later did I learn to look for that sudden illuminating smile which gave the necessary reassurance.'

ST. MARTIN'S HIGH SCHOOL.

Term Record for Brenda Mortiboy   Form IV.B.   Autumn Term, 1927.

	1st MONTH.	2nd MONTH.
Scripture.	Fairly good.	Good.
English.	Good.	Not so good lately.
French	Fairly good.	Fairly good. More thought needed
Latin.	Promising work. With thought o can should do well	Disappointing lately.
History.	Work variable. Is capable of doing well.	Fairly good. Brenda still needs to work hard.
Arithmetic.		Good on the whole.
Algebra.	} Very fair.	Only fair: - more careful effort
Geometry.		needed
Geography.	Generally works well.	Not so good of late.
Botany or Nature Study.	Very fair.	Fair.
General Report from Form Mistress.	A satisfactory month's work.	Rather disappointing on the whole. Brenda does not seem to have made very definite progress. I think she is apt to dream.
Parent's Signature.	ow: Mortiboy	C M. Mortiboy

Termly report card (Fletcher)

During the last full year at Charing Cross, St Martin's House set out to raise money to have a picture of the school drawn by a Mr Alfred Bennett. The previous year, the House had raised money and commissioned Mr Bennett to draw St Martin-in-the-Fields Church at a cost of £9. The picture had been presented to the school and was so well received that the House decided to go ahead with the new commission. The enterprising House went on to have Christmas cards and calendars reproduced from the drawing. Later, these proved popular with present and past girls who wanted a souvenir of their old school.

To raise the money, an entertainment reported as 'quite successful' was organised. Favours for the Oxford and Cambridge boat race were sold, and copies of two crossword puzzles, compiled by members of the House, sold for a penny each. But a sale in the summer term was the greatest success, which House prefects Gwen Botten and Clarice Kippin described:

> 'The chief attraction was no doubt the Cake and Candy Stall, and the girls in charge were kept very busy with all their customers. Also the Tea, which was served in the Music Room, drew great crowds, and the Flower and Fancy Stalls were well patronised. Two raffles added to the enjoyment of the occasion, [the prizes being] an' enormous Mimosa, which had just won a prize at the big Flower Show in the Horticultural Hall, and an attractive kitten given by Eileen Mackay, who spent a busy afternoon protecting "Martin" from the fervent embraces of admirers. The plant fell to the lot of G. Vernon, and Miss Gordon-Ewen won the kitten.'

Miss Gordon Ewen, who taught history, also helped Miss Bannister with some of the mounting secretarial work.

In 1927 Miss Gordon Ewen handed over her secretarial duties to Miss Smyth, the first full-time school secretary to be appointed. In addition, Miss Smyth relieved Miss Bannister of much of her clerical work, as for many years she had been Clerk to the Governors.

Although it was hoped that the new building at Tulse Hill would be completed by autumn 1927, the year was creeping by. On winter afternoons gas lamps still cast their uneven yellow light across the classrooms, and older girls began to wonder if they would ever be part of the new modern school.

At the beginning of 1928, when the girls assembled in the drill room, they were told the move would take place in the Easter holidays. But even the Head Girl doubted the time had really come. What finally convinced her was 'a simple piece of string', because as she wandered into the music room she saw a bundle of books neatly tied together, and with a thrill of excitement realised she really would be spending her last term in school at Tulse Hill.

3. Tulse Hill: 1928 - 1939

The Staff, the Sixth, the Upper Fifth,
Were working High and low;
They listed, sorted, labelled, tied,
The books, row after row.
"If ever this is done," they said,
"To Tulse Hill we can go."

"If seven maids with seven strings
Tie them for half-a-year,
Do you suppose," Miss Thomas said,
"We'll ever get it clear?"
"We doubt it," said the harassed Sixth,
And shed a bitter tear.

The Staff, the Sixth, the Upper Fifth,
Worked on to stem the stream
With miles of string and quarts of gum
And paper by the ream;
And still the books appeared and still
No fewer did they seem.

(Part of a poem in the school magazine by an anonymous writer,with apologies to
Lewis Carroll)

There was much to do. 'How we tied and labelled, packed and re-packed!' commented the Head Girl, Maria Curtis. For staff and senior girls it was a hectic time, and through it all the life of the school flowed on. 'Teachers taught, girls learnt, played and did homework as usual,' said Maria.

The previous year, Miss Bannister had written in her *School Notes* in the magazine:

'One practical point I wish to bring to the attention of every St Martin's girl. Remember that we are moving into a quiet neighbourhood at Tulse Hill and that we must impose upon ourselves a very high standard of courtesy towards our neighbours, and of dignified and quiet manners on our way to and from school. We aim at reaching a high academic standard in our new school. Let us also aim at a high standard of courtesy, good manners and consideration for others.'

57

Although the charm of an earlier generation was being left behind and a new era in the school's life was beginning, courtesy and consideration would not be forgotten. In 1928 Miss Bannister wrote:

'The change is bound to be all to the good so long as we keep firmly in our minds the highest ideals of our old school traditions, and our love for the school wherever it is housed. We must aim at a spirit of harmonious co-operation and friendly peace, taking care not to become an unwieldy community because of our rapidly increasing numbers, but a busy hive of happy industry.'

And a busy hive of happy industry it was, for during the Easter holidays staff and senior girls worked on, this time unpacking boxes, arranging books and getting the school ready for not just the 150 who would be continuing from Charing Cross, but nearly as many new girls from the neighbourhood.

The day before the summer term started, the band of helpers returned to learn the geography of the school, so they could become guides for the rest of the girls in the vast new surroundings. Guides were needed to usher classes from one form to another, helpers were needed to lay the tables for lunch, to answer questions and to reassure. All these duties older girls happily accomplished as they, too, learnt their bearings.

With the move to Tulse Hill came a complete change of uniform. No longer would girls wear the thick pleated navy tunic, for now there was a plain dark brown one over a beige, square-necked blouse. For the summer term a wide cream panama hat was worn, and in winter a brown velour with 'flame' and brown band depicting the school badge. A dark brown blazer, with badge emblazoning the pocket, replaced the navy blue, while for prefects narrow, flame braid adorned the edges. And no longer would the thick pleated tunic and woollen stockings be worn for sports; instead, despite loss of dignity particularly for older girls, only blouse and dark brown school knickers would be worn.

On that first morning girls stood anxiously or excitedly by the top netball court, waiting for the lower cloakroom door to be opened. Each clutched her shoe bag, embroidered with her name, containing her indoor shoes and gym shoes. As soon as the door was opened, prefects directed the girls to rows and rows of empty pegs, soon to be filled with brand new blazers, hats and dangling shoe bags.

The girls were then taken to the spacious gymnasium, with its wall bars between French windows that opened out on to a paved area that ran along the side of the building. Huge ropes were fixed to the ceiling, and around the walls stood more pieces of apparatus. Once assembled in the gym the girls were divided into their forms. Afterwards, in batches, they were escorted up the wide concrete stairs following dark blue, then dark green half-tiled walls to pristine classrooms.

More blue or green tiles adorned the walls of the corridors and classrooms, but in form one, orange tiles were interspersed with small blackboards at pupil height. This classroom looked down over gardens, flowering bushes and fruit trees on either side of the netball and tennis courts to the field below. An unknown Old Girl was later to describe the view from the first form window:

> 'Within five miles of Charing Cross one can look down across the school field to trees which completely hide the main road, and see beyond them only a high green hill dotted with trees — hardly a chimney in sight.'

The other classrooms, with tall windows and wide sills, ran down the length of the new extension on two floors, with the gymnasium

View over the school field (Fletcher)

59

and cloakrooms below. Opaque glass on the inner corridor walls added to the light and airy appearance. New to the girls from Charing Cross were the facilities at the top of the building, which Marjorie Cheeseman in the lower fifth described:

> 'At the top of the school is the Art Room, a beautiful room which has proper lighting arrangements; the special desks have every convenience for drawing and painting, with a ledge on which to rest the drawing board. Adjoining this are the Science Rooms, which are most interesting, although we do not yet know the use of all the fittings. Next to them is the Botany Room. Here, large tables are used instead of desks, at which four girls can sit. Then there is the Lecture Room where we have singing lessons. On the same floor as all these rooms are the Rest Room and the Library.'

Some city girls had been left behind as it was too far for them to travel. Other girls, who had walked or gone by bus or train to Charing Cross, now cycled down to Tulse Hill to join new girls from the neighbourhood. An endowment fund made provision for 'special scholarships for suitable candidates from the parish of St Martin's', otherwise girls from Charing Cross paid three pounds ten shillings per term, and girls starting at Tulse Hill paid four guineas. But old or new, all girls mingled happily together in their unaccustomed space.

The school had been given many gifts, including valuable prints of Westminster and central London, and historic prints to fill bare walls in the classrooms and along the corridors. The old oil painting of an original pupil, which had moved with the school in its many homes, was cleaned and renovated. It now hung above the stage in the assembly hall, which appeared so large compared with the old drill room. Other ornate-framed paintings of past benefactors, including that of Francis Caryl painted in 1775, adorned the walls of the hall.

Miss Frere, one of the school governors, 'gave her own beautiful grand piano to grace the hall', and for many years it was to dominate its own special corner by the stage. Water colours and a comfortable sofa were donated for Miss Bannister's 'sitting room' (office); and the library was presented with many old and new books to add to its existing collection.

One prized item which travelled down to Tulse Hill with the

school was Miss Pulée's fireplace. Several years before, through contributions from governors, staff and girls old and new, the sculptured fireplace, depicting St Martin and the beggar, had been given to the school in memory of Miss Pulée. The fireplace now took up its new position in the school library, housed in the old part of the building.

The library overlooked the front garden through two tall windows, one on either side of a narrow glazed door leading to a small balcony above the entrance porch. From money raised by producing and selling a calendar, the original small collection of books had come into existence during World War 1. In the early twenties the shelves contained nearly 600 books in the lending library and 250 for reference. The number had steadily increased, through LCC grants and various gifts. To prolong the life of the books some girls became skilful at bookbinding. Others spent their lunch hour sewing fiction books into covers of 'brown holland'.

Once at Tulse Hill, many more books were added and it took time to sort and catalogue the whole collection. Each class had its own 'library' of fiction books, but because of the small numbers girls were only allowed to borrow one book at a time. Betty Lee, a sub-librarian, wrote:

> 'At our old school in Charing Cross Road, the reference library was hardly known to the Junior school, and the seniors could only borrow books through the staff; but now, even the third forms may sit there and read in their spare time. In spite of our pride in our "new" library, we are quite aware that some sections are greatly in need of more books, a fact which we hope time will remedy.'

With books in place, lessons in progress and brown-clothed girls filing through the long corridors, the school gradually settled into its new home. Extra teaching staff were taken on at the start of the summer term and the syllabus was broadened. But new building and new routines did not diminish the traditions of the past.

Mr and Mrs Jones were appointed caretaker and cook, and Mrs Jones' sister, who was always known as 'Blake', became the housekeeper. They had a flat in the old part of the building and remained with the school for many years. Mr Sturmey the gardener, who lived in a cottage in the grounds, completed the initial auxiliary staff. Later, groundsmen and kitchen staff were to come and go, while Mr and Mrs Jones and Blake stayed on. At mid-morning break time, to swell school funds, Blake was to be found in the pavilion — or cookery room in bad weather — selling chocolate biscuits or apples for a penny each and oranges for a penny-halfpenny.

Having taken the entrance exam at Charing Cross, Joan Nurse arrived at Tulse Hill two weeks late for the summer term, because her brother had had scarlet fever. In remembering those early days Joan said:

> 'When I arrived, they seemed to have forgotten about me, and no one was sure which form I was allocated to. I ended up in Lower III. All the girls were older than me — as I later found out — in most cases by two years. I knew what *proper* school would be like as for more than a year I had been an avid reader of *Schoolgirls' Own*; I decided to be like the naughtiest girl in the Fourth at Morcove.
>
> 'Within a couple of days it was made very clear to me that this was *not* what school was really like; not only by the staff, but by the other girls. Those who already knew me, either from my previous school or from living nearby, disowned me. It was then realized I was in the wrong form, and I was moved to the Second Form, where I had the sense to forget Morcove and start afresh. The Second Form was presided over by Miss Miles who among other subjects taught us Elocution — "How now brown cow" and "Full fathom five thy father lies".'

Not long after Joan Nurse started at St Martin's, the school was officially opened.

Wednesday the 23rd of May 1928 was designated 'Opening Day', and from the start of that first summer term everything led towards this special event, when the school was to be officially opened by the Duchess of York (the present Queen Mother).

Excitement grew as each form filed out of their classroom to assemble in the hall. The younger girls packed into the gallery at the back, peering over the balcony to watch visitors arrive. Tickets had previously been issued and parents, Old Girls and friends, who streamed in through the front entrance, passed several policemen before handing their tickets to the uniformed school porter. Wet umbrellas and mackintoshes were left in a cloakroom, then senior girls escorted the visitors to their reserved seats.

Accompanying the rain pattering on the windows, an excited buzz of voices filled the hall — until 3 o'clock when the buzz abruptly stopped. A lookout had signalled that the distinguished party was heading towards the hall. But one small girl, Audrey Kidby, was not in the hall, for as she was later to write:

'While all this was going on, my mother was dressing me in the uniform worn by one of the original pupils of St Martin's. This consisted of an ankle-length, navy serge frock, white starched cap, apron and "tippet", and yellow silk, elbow-length mittens. With the exception of the frock, all of these garments had actually belonged to one of the children who had attended the school when it was founded. The clothes were all beautifully made by hand. To complete the costume I wore a sprig of myrtle tucked into the front of my belt.

'When I was ready, I was led down to the "Green Room" next to the Assembly Hall, and there I waited, clutching the bouquet which I was to present to the Duchess of York. Several press reporters and photographers were in attendance, each of whom asked me — to my surprise — whether I felt nervous at meeting so great a personage. In fact, I was asked so many times that I began to wonder whether I ought to be a little frightened. As it was, I was enjoying every minute of it.

'Just after 3pm, the Duchess arrived. Accompanied by Miss Bannister, Miss Humphry, Chairman of the Governors, the Rev Dick Sheppard and the Rev Pat McCormick, then past and present Vicars of St Martin-in-the-Fields, and other school governors, her Royal Highness took her place on the platform. After the National Anthem had been sung, I presented my bouquet of pink rosebuds to the Duchess. Our Head Girl, Marie Curtis, presented Miss Humphry with a bouquet of sweet peas, and Joan Kent, one of the smaller girls, gave Miss Bannister a bouquet of tea roses.'

In declaring the school open, the Duchess wished it every success in its beautiful new home, and said she was confident that St Martin's would maintain the high standard of education and character-training for which it had always been well known.

Before leaving the hall for tea with the official party, the Duchess was presented with a small posy of flowers 'for the baby Princess Elizabeth', by Joan Kent in modern gym tunic, and Audrey Kidby in her ancient costume. After a tour of the school, including at her own request, laboratories, art room and kitchen, the Duchess passed

The Duchess of York receiving a bouquet (Bourhill)

along the lower corridor lined with cheering girls. Three cheers were called, and as the Duchess reached the high-domed vestibule in the entrance hall she turned, waved and gave her gentle smile. The cheering continued until the official party had left the school.

With the building officially opened, a new routine began to be established. As the summer term progressed, tennis, cricket and rounders were introduced now the school had its own facilities. Heats were run during the week before Sports Day, with the finals on a gloriously sunny afternoon at the end of June. More races had been added, including slow bicycle, tennis, one for visitors and another for the Preparatory Department.

Refreshments were served in the pavilion for the girls, while parents and friends had tea in the 'spacious gymnasium'. At one point there were anxious moments when the tea room was invaded by several hundreds at the same time. But fathers became waiters and mothers and Old Girls were 'found acting as extra kitchen maids', so all went well.

As work continued towards end of term exams, the first term in the new school building seemed to race by. Joan Nurse recalled:

> 'This first term must have been one of sorting out teething troubles, and the next term there was a major reconstruction of the lower forms. Two new forms were added at the bottom: the Kindergarten and the Transition. A few girls, myself among them, went into Lower III under the quite formidable Miss McClemens.
>
> 'Miss McClemens taught us Arithmetic and English, I imagine very well, but what I remember best is her capacity for storytelling. She also took us for a two hour session of needlework on Friday afternoons. While we worked she told us or read us stories, and I remember waiting anxiously each week for the next instalment of *The Magnolia Tree*.
>
> 'In my schooldays teachers had to leave if they married. An exception was made for Miss McClemens, who was allowed to stay on after she became Mrs Davies. We assumed it was because Mr Davies was disabled. To us, Miss McClemens was in any case 'old' — even now I cannot imagine how old, but at least forty!'

After her marriage in Canterbury Cathedral, Mrs Davies stayed with the school for many years and was remembered for her intuitive teaching:

> 'When she told us the story of Thor she stood on her desk shaking her arms. We were delighted,' remembered Jean Walton (née Hey).

The Junior School, or Preparatory Department, as the classes up to lower third were called, used the lower of the two main cloakrooms. Each morning, girls would hang up their coats and hats and change from their outdoor lace-up shoes into softer, one-barred indoor shoes. Prayers for the juniors were held in the gym, where the girls sat cross-legged on the floor in three semi-circular rows. Miss Miles, the head of the Junior School, conducted the short assembly and gave out notices, and Mrs Davies played the piano for the hymn. Three more teachers sat on chairs facing the horseshoe of small girls.

At the same time, Prayers for the Senior School, conducted by Miss Bannister, were held in the main hall. On Fridays the orchestra played and one day a week there was a collection for charity. While girls and staff waited for Miss Bannister to arrive, Miss Copland, the music teacher, played quiet classical pieces on the grand piano — a much appreciated routine that was to last for many years.

At lunch time, hands had to be washed before the Junior School filed into the cookery room near the gym, to sit at long tables headed by a teacher. Afterwards, the youngest ones rested on the floor in their classroom while they listened to a story. But any girl who was too young to stay the whole day could be taken home before lunch.

Going up to the upper third in the autumn term of 1928 meant the girls from lower third were joined by a new intake of girls, and all were divided into two parallel classes. Once in the Senior School the curriculum broadened. Classes moved quietly from room to room for different lessons, instead of staying in the same form room as before. Bells rang and classes changed in orderly files; no talking, no running in the corridors or on the stairs. But being in the Senior School meant the occasional outing and membership of the school societies.

The long-founded (1913) Literary and Debating Society continued to hold its regular meetings once the new term started. Over the years many subjects had been covered including 'Civilization is more a bane than a blessing', 'It is impossible to be too broadminded' and the old favourite, 'Homework should be abolished'. That autumn term, debating resumed with 'A holiday in a caravan is everyway preferable to one in a boarding house' and 'To be well dressed is not worth the trouble and expense involved'. After a 'sharp debate' and 'heated argument' both motions were carried.

Membership of the Classical Society, which had formed just before the move to Tulse Hill, was for girls from the upper fourth to the sixth form who were learning Latin. The society joined the Inter-Schools Classical Club and visited James Allen Girls' School for a meeting on excavations in Surrey, Kent and Sussex, with illustrations of Roman remains.

On another occasion, Miss Millburn, the headmistress of Northampton Girls' School, showed original photographs on the 'epidiascope' of excavations at Mycenae. The meetings prompted the hope that return visits by other schools could now be made to St Martin's.

The junior branch of the League of Nations held many of its regular meetings in the lunch time, when members discussed the importance of the league's work and the need for arbitration instead of war. War was uppermost in their minds when a group of branch members went to the Queen's Hall to hear Lloyd George speak on disarmament.

Added to these societies now came the Music Club and the Historical Society. In subsequent years more would follow — the Science Club; Le Cercle Français; Gardening Club; and Country Dancing Society. Each one, with enthusiasm, widened the horizons of its members.

Autumn terms in any school are busy terms, and as events wound their way towards Christmas, choosing items for the annual school entertainment had to be fitted in around the full timetable. Small sketches, poems, dances and songs were meticulously practised, with each class making a contribution.

Year by year, authentic costumes and much hard work had come together in the final, fleeting production, when parents and friends had crowded into the old drill room. And when the fifth and sixth forms paid a visit to Mary Datchelor's School to see *Alcestis*, it had emphasised the difficulty St Martin's had in staging a full production. In 1926, although the sixth form had produced 'two delightful performances of *Quality Street*', lack of space meant that the school watched in the afternoon and visitors watched in the evening. But now, the spacious new hall provided more opportunities in a much grander setting.

Several visits each year had been made to nearby London Theatres for matinée performances, including *Oliver Cromwell*, *La Misanthrope*, *The Rivals* and many Shakespearean plays. Despite the greater distance to be travelled, parties of girls and staff continued to visit the Old Vic and other London theatres from Tulse Hill, although less frequently.

'Dramatic Readings' by the British Empire Shakespearean Society at the Strand Theatre had been particularly interesting in Charing Cross days, because a St Martin's Old Girl, known at school as Ethel McGlinchy, had joined the cast. As Fabia Drake, she stayed with the company and went on to do a successful tour of Canada and America with the Stratford-upon-Avon Shakespeare Memorial Company. Newspapers wrote of her 'winning laurels on all sides and going from one success to another'.

Fabia Drake returned to the school, in its new building, to present a trophy to the winners of a drama competition, and Jean Scotzin (née Austen) well remembered the occasion:

> 'A Drama Competition was inaugurated for forms upper third to the sixth and we, the youngest form taking part, did a skit on Macbeth. With what relish did Lady Macbeth cry "Out, damned spot, out I say" — damn being a pretty strong word at the time! We were delighted to be declared the winners and were awarded the trophy (a statuette of Peter Pan as depicted in Kensington Gardens) by Fabia Drake, the actress and Old Girl.'

More ambitious productions could now be undertaken, and the newly-formed Operatic Society began rehearsals for *Hiawatha*, which proved to be the first of many successes. On these occasions members of all Houses came together for the productions.

With the move out of the City, the London charities were not forgotten, and several times during the autumn term collections of clothes were delivered to Ranyard House. Secondhand toys were also collected, and one patient form teacher commented, 'Room S began to resemble a toy bazaar.' The toys, together with those specially made by the Houses, were finally displayed in the hall before being delivered to the Ranyard Mission, who distributed them to needy children in London.

End of term tests could not subdue the pre-Christmas excitement, and Kathleen Burbidge, in the upper third, summed up the feelings on the last day of that first autumn term at Tulse Hill:

> 'Papers are rustling as girls tie up their books, and doors are opening and shutting as messengers come in and out. Mistresses are busily finishing their last important checking, and girls are chattering eagerly about the coming

holiday. The painted letter box, where Christmas cards are lying, looks festive on the cupboard. Snow on the ground outside perfectly fits in with the season. Now the letter box is being opened at last, and girls eagerly await the "postmen". Cards are admired and thanks are being given with fervour.

'Lost property is being brought round and a girl without a halfpenny to pay for a fine and who wants her goods, is in a pretty situation! At this time thoughts of lessons become intolerable; and a girl who has slacked envies those who have stars and optimes to show for their term's work. Now cheering and clapping is becoming louder and louder as the results of the work of each House are read out. Our good time is drawing to a close, and girls are saying au revoir to those whom they will probably not see for several weeks. "Good bye, Joan, don't forget to write." "Betty, I'll see you on Monday; don't be late." "Good bye! Good bye! A Happy Christmas!".'

Clutching their bulging shoe bags, books, cards and presents, girls left the school, discussing the term's House results in friendly rivalry.

There was always friendly rivalry, particularly over inter-House sports matches. Netball still featured prominently, and now there was no undersized court to play on — to which other schools had strongly objected. Instead, three full-sized courts accommodated first and second school teams, with matches played through the autumn and spring terms.

A portion of ground on the edge of the field had been divided so that each House could have its own garden. Docks, groundsel and other weeds had taken hold, but during the summer term staff and older girls stayed behind after school to dig and prepare the soil. Weeds were pulled up, plants were planted and the 'pleasant sounds of laughter and happy voices rang in the garden while the work went on'.

For Pearl Bourhill (née Gosnell) gardening suddenly became a new and enjoyable activity when she was only seven. As she struggled with her sums one morning:

'Miss Bannister came into the maths lesson to say that it was such a lovely day we could all go out to help weed the gardens.'

As more girls joined the school, a sixth House was created called St Christopher's. Again the new House was made up from girls in each of the existing Houses, and they soon showed their allegiance to St Christopher's at the regular meetings held on Mondays after school. Even so, St Christopher's was only to last for two years because the House system was to come to an end due to the pressure of increased work. But until that time House activities flourished.

A great moment for the school came when a 'wireless set' was installed in the hall, with extensions to five classes. Miss Bannister referred to it as 'one of our most valuable possessions'. A representative from the BBC and the Chief Woman Inspector of the Board of Education visited the school, to see how the set was used.

When the London Naval Conference was relayed from the Royal Gallery in the House of Commons, girls from the upper fourth upwards were allowed to listen to the wireless in the school hall.

> 'We sat round the dinner tables which were laid for dinner as there wouldn't have been enough time to lay them afterwards,' commented Joan Nash from the lower fifth.

King George V opened the conference, followed by delegates from America, France, Italy, Japan, Canada and Australia all expressing the desire for disarmament and peace, a hope that was paramount in those uncertain days.

With the new well-equipped gymnasium, gym lessons had become popular. Inter-form gymnastic competitions were held in the spring term, when the senior competition was judged by Miss Chamberlain of the Grey Coat School, Westminster. Miss Chamberlain 'considered the work shown was promising, but not yet sufficiently good for St Martin's wonderfully equipped new gymnasium.' The winning junior team received a framed photograph of the Dunfermline Challenge Statuette, depicting a girl in an 'easy and correct standing position'. The advice of the judge, Mrs Gill from Streatham County Secondary School, was to 'stretch ourselves from skull to tail'.

Remembering her own gym lessons, Joan Nurse said:

> 'Miss Trost spoke of the necessity for exercise even at That Time of the Month, and of the need to wear bust-bodices. . .We found this remark hilarious and a term our grandmothers might have used.'

Hockey, which had tentatively started in the first autumn term at Tulse Hill, now became established. To get a better understanding of the game, a party of fifth- and sixth-formers went to Central Hall, Westminster, to see a film on the tactics of the game. They were accompanied by Miss Pummel, one of the three games mistresses, and Miss Smyth, the school secretary. The President of the All England Women's Hockey Association, Miss Pollard, talked about the opposition that the first women players had met. Further hints on attacking and defending to improve the game were given by notable hockey players, and the party left full of enthusiasm.

With this encouragement, the fifth and sixth forms established a school hockey team for inter-schools matches. At first games were played between Streatham College, Clear View School, Streatham Hill and Peckham Secondary, but later other nearby schools were added to the fixture list as the teams became more proficient.

Once a week after school, Miss Smyth, who at one time had played hockey for England, coached the upper fourth. And soon hockey and netball became obligatory for the upper and lower fourth, while the fifth and sixth could choose either game. Sometimes hockey matches and practice had to be cancelled because of bad weather which affected the field. But after treatment with 'sand and cinders' the field was soon regularly back in use again. Enthusiasm spread and practice was important as Eileen State, the school hockey captain, reported:

> 'The field was available for practice during the dinner hours, under the supervision of certain senior girls. Although a few keen members of the XIs are especially to be commended for their enthusiasm in attending regularly, it is felt that others should have taken this opportunity of improving their strokes, when time could not always be allowed for this in the games lessons.'

In the autumn term, of 1931, it was proudly announced that Eileen State had been chosen to play centre-half-back for the Surrey Junior County hockey team.

The following year a team went to Merton Abbey to take part in the Inter-schools Hockey Tournament. And when girls from the first XI attended the Surrey Junior Hockey Trials, one girl was picked for the reserve team and another for the 'further reserve'.

With the ending of the school House system, sports matches became inter-form, and some matches were played against staff and Old Girls' teams. In ending the Houses, Miss Bannister explained in the school magazine:

> 'For some time past it has become increasingly difficult to fit in the numerous social activities of the school. We were obliged to face the fact that the chief aim of a wisely run school must be to arrange its programme in such a way that the attainment of a high standard of work should be possible without undue overstrain for staff or girls. To speak plainly, work must be the first consideration.
>
> 'The School Houses have certainly performed a most useful function, especially while we were a smaller school in Charing Cross. But our many out-of-school activities have made too large a demand of the time of Prefects, and at a meeting of the House Constitution, consisting of House Mistresses and Prefects, a large majority voted for the disbanding of the School Houses. There is still plenty of scope for the many active spirits in the school, as we shall still have a Literary and Dramatic Society, an Historic Society, a Science Society, the School Choir, and a Folk Dance Society — to say nothing of the Games Club.'

It is significant that Miss Bannister ended these *School Notes* by writing:

> 'Many of the older girls realize that the country is passing through a most difficult crisis. It is more essential than ever that every girl should be qualified, not only to earn her own living, but to become a thoughtful and helpful daughter and citizen. I ask every girl to remember that her parents are faced just now with added difficulties, and that it is her plain duty to try to help them in every possible way, and, in particular, to take home the best possible report at the end of term.'

With these stirring words maintaining the standards of the school, firm discipline permeated school life as an underlying, often unspoken presence.

Detentions meant attendance on Wednesday afternoons; normally this was free time for younger girls. For older ones the afternoon was devoted to hockey and netball in winter, or tennis and rounders in summer. A double-detention on a Wednesday meant a visit to the headmistress, 'a matter of particular dread'.

Despite this apprehension — a fear which most school children had — Miss Bannister was remembered by Barbara Lafrance (née Nex) as a 'kindly yet somewhat remote lady'. Barbara recalled Miss Bannister sometimes sitting in the small summerhouse, watching as girls went by to the field, and that:

> 'Miss Bannister was also often to be found at the front gate of the school as we left for home. She would give a gentle smile and a nod of approval — providing we had our hats on straight and our gloves! Decorum was the order of the day. We were learning we had a certain image of the school and ourselves which we were supposed to uphold. Outside the school, needless to say, once safely down the hill we weren't quite so neat, but it was all good training.'

The good training included walking in the street no more than two abreast, and always standing back to let an adult pass. Eating or drinking in the street were unheard of, so too was dropping litter. If any one of these rules was occasionally broken, the offender could be reported by a member of the public who would recognise the distinctive uniform.

Behaviour was impeccable at lunch time too, remembered Joan Nurse:

> 'Tables seated eight and each was headed by a mistress. One girl acted as monitor, fetching the food for her table, and the older girls also provided this service for the younger tables. One had the alternative of going home to lunch or bringing a packed lunch from home. . .The choice of bringing a packed lunch was almost certainly due to faddiness rather than parents' means, but there was indeed a feeling that the "in-crowd" ate the school lunch even if they hated it.'

In 1931 there had been twenty girls in the upper fifth taking Cambridge School Certificate examinations. By 1932 the number had increased to sixty, and London General Schools Certificate (GSC) exams were introduced, replacing Cambridge. A credit in five 'suitable subjects' obtained Matriculation. At the same time the sixth-form syllabus was widened to cover Higher Certificate courses, individual modern languages for the Royal Society of Arts and training in typing and shorthand. Examination results in 1933 reflected this broader coverage and enlarged sixth form.

Forty-two girls had been working on individual timetables, preparing for university, training colleges, 'dispensing courses', civil service, secretarial posts and business courses. Because of this increase, more prefects were appointed and the 'green room' beside the hall was transformed into a prefects' room. A school committee was also formed, and Elizabeth Dadd gave the following report:

> 'It was felt that it would help the school to achieve freedom if it were given more responsibility and opportunity for self-discipline. Realising how much we learn from one another's point of view, we have made the Committee as representative as possible. It consists of four *ex-officio* members, Miss Bannister, Miss Thomas, the Head Girl and Deputy Head Girl, three elected members of the Staff, one prefect, one Vice-Prefect, and two representatives from Lower IV to Upper VI. The Upper III send representatives in the summer term.'

This reflected the more progressive approach to education which had gradually emerged. Gone was the narrow view of 'mechanical obedience', instead had come 'self-realization' based on ideas of Froebel, Montessori, Dewey and others before them. And the aim that *learning is doing* had spread.

Eileen Fyffe, daughter of actor Will Fyffe, took 'learning is doing' to the extreme when she re-styled her school hat.

> 'She arrived at school one morning wearing a hat that resembled a flying saucer,' said Jeanne Scotzin. 'She had lopped about two inches off the crown and then sewn the brim back on. The result was very fashionable and so far as I recall there were no repercussions!'

Eileen also appeared at school with her hair permed, which was unheard of when girls either had a straight bob, plaits or naturally curly hair.

It can't have been every girl's choice of activity, on the last day of the spring term in 1934, to hear a lecture called 'Smoke'. Even so, girls filed into the hall and waited expectantly. 'The talk proved to be pure propaganda on the evils of using coal for domestic fires and the advantages of coke,' commented sixth-former Kathleen Burbidge. With thoughts more on the end of term than on the three great dangers – damage to buildings, loss of by-products and lack of sunshine which could cause rickets in children – the girls sat patiently through the lecture.

Far more enjoyable, for groups from the fifth and sixth, was the first school visit to Wimbledon the following term. They watched with delight well-known tennis players of the day, the Misses Round, Jacobs, Scriven, Palfrey and Babcock, and determined to improve their own tennis playing.

The first Founders' Day was celebrated in February 1935. It started with a short service in the school hall, then followed talks covering the early history of the school, the gradual development of women's education, the role of school governors and developments since the school moved to Tulse Hill. In a report, Margaret Pellow of the upper sixth said:

> 'The School then sang the new "Song for Founders' Day", written for the occasion by Miss Richmond and set to music by Miss Copland. The first part of the celebration ended with the school marching past the School Flag.'

Who's for Tennis (Fletcher)

75

Celebrations continued into the afternoon with sports displays. Finally, the staff acted out the 'highly amusing, hypothetical scenario' of what would happen if teachers were replaced with 'radio education through loud speakers'. The following year started the annual tradition of celebrating Founders' Day at St Martin-in-the-Fields Church, which always ended with rousing sounds of the school song.

By November 1935, a general election was causing the usual stir throughout the country. Ripples were felt at St Martin's when a mock election was staged — the first of many school elections. Three sixth form girls were chosen to represent the main parties, and much canvassing and many speeches took place. Two lower sixth-formers reported:

> 'The walls of the gymnasium were covered with arresting and highly coloured placards; small groups of excited canvassers paraded the corridors displaying their party labels, seeking to convince the wavering mob. . . Canvassing continued through the morning, and during the afternoon many blackboards were decorated with encouraging slogans, written in brilliant-coloured chalk. Thursday was polling day, and voting took place in the hall at recreation, where the ballot boxes were presided over by the Upper VI.'

Another innovation had been a ten-day international holiday to stay with a Belgian school near Brussels. A group from St Martin's was joined by girls from Chatham County School and Streatham County Secondary School. A corporate report by St Martin's travellers said:

> 'Our bedrooms were extremely comfortable with large windows, wash hand basins and armchairs; especially popular were the showers. We could play games in the ground behind the hostel or table-tennis in the vestibule, or dance to the radio-gramophone. The Belgian girls were very jolly. . . What they found most disturbing about us was our uniform. . . they then saw us ready for games. They were amazed. That a mistress also should wear this uniform [gym tunics] seemed incomprehensible. . . But any differences between English and Belgian girls were slight. It was a delightful surprise to find how alike we really were.
>
> 'Perhaps the most exciting privilege we enjoyed was being allowed to see the balloon in which Professor Picard attempted to reach the stratosphere. But this was not all; Professor Picard himself came, and with delightful modesty explained his ascent and also showed us his new balloon, in the making, in one of the University laboratories.'

For girls unused to travelling abroad, their crowded Easter visit was a remarkable and memorable holiday.

Staying at an Amsterdam Youth Hostel enabled a party of fifty-six, from several British schools, to cover a wide area and meet many Dutch boys and girls. One object of this holiday was to visit the Permanent Court of International Justice at the Hague. The party found the visit 'most impressive' as the Peace Palace included contributions from many countries, including a stained-glass window from Britain.

A tour of the Rhineland in 1937, with boys from Midhurst Grammar School, was hosted by members of the Hitler Youth. Under the meticulous organisation of the Hitler Youth leader in charge of foreign guests, the party experienced the delights of new foods in Cologne, a visit to Heidelberg Castle and the narrow cobbled streets of Frankfurt. War was not envisaged by the boys and girls from England, or by their hosts, the Hitler Youth, whose members were unaware they were being trained for military service. One of the group expressed her thoughts when she wrote:

> 'We shall never forget how on the last night at Frankfurt, their voices rang through the night as they stood below our window, with their guitars to serenade us!'

The party moved on to Rudessheim where they were 'struck by the militaristic propaganda which was usually hardly perceptible'. The unknown writer finished her report by saying:

> 'We are corresponding with the boys and girls we met in Germany, and we hope that a friendly relationship will continue to grow between the two countries.'

Sadly, this was not to be and it was the last holiday in Germany for many years.

A major event of 1937 was the Coronation, when a party of sixty girls travelled by train from Tulse Hill to Victoria Station. By 10.30 they were lining the Victoria Embankment, waiting patiently with 47,000 children. Members of staff and stewards from the LCC handed round packets of crisps and cartons of milk, when strict observance of 'no eating in the street' was temporarily forgotten. Somehow, the crowds managed to sit on the pavement to eat their packed lunches, as time slowly dragged by. In her account of the visit, Greta Thornley from the upper fourth concluded:

> 'At last came the procession of the day. The Royal procession. Oh how marvellous it was! First came the Duchesses of Kent and Gloucester. . . Next came Queen Mary and the two little Princesses, followed by the state carriage of gold carrying their Majesties the King and Queen. . . The Dukes of Kent and Gloucester . . . rode side by side on horseback. Troops ended the procession, which thrilled us all and which will remain as a great memory to us all for ever.'

Floodlit London was a Coronation attraction for Joan Duffell, of the lower fifth, who recalled:

> 'Crowds of people thronged the stations, for trains were the only method of transport in the West End. I edged my way out of a tube exit near Oxford Street, having decided to see Selfridges at any cost.'

London was awash with colour, bright lights and cheering people as Joan moved with the crowds, finally ending at Piccadilly Circus:

> 'At Piccadilly the humour of the crowd was more boisterous. Bands of young people with balloons, paper caps, whistles and streamers, singing at the top of their voices, marched round the circus, while harassed policemen vainly issued orders through loud speakers.'

After the excitement of the Coronation subsided, journeys to the West End continued when a small party of six girls visited the House of Commons, and a large party of girls from St Martin's joined other London schools and youth organisations at Westminster Abbey for the Empire Youth Service.

The regular Founders' Day Service at St Martin-in-the-Fields Church had now been established, and each February the school travelled to Trafalgar Square in 'seven private omnibuses'. Some smaller girls sat three to a double seat in the full but orderly buses. The choir and the school orchestra performed at the services which were conducted by the Reverend Pat McCormick, and in 1938 the Lord Bishop of Kensington gave an inspiring address on the history of the school, showing the contrasts between 1738 and 1938. But more changes in the life of the school were ahead.

From the moment Hitler became Chancellor political tensions had steadily grown. Germany's annexing of the Rhineland and Austria, and the blatant flouting of the Treaty of Versailles by continued re-armament, had caused growing alarm. For many children in Britain the inherent dangers had largely passed them by, but with the imminent threat to Czechoslovakia in 1938, came plans for evacuating children from London. As the threat of war came nearer, St Martin's contingency plans were drawn up, with preparations for immediate evacuation should war be declared. Later Miss Bannister was to write:

> 'The school resembled the left-luggage department of a busy railway station and even in that anxious time we found much amusement in such incidents as the very bulky luggage of very small people, found on inspection to contain dolls, toys and many treasures intended presumably to add to the enjoyment of a delightful holiday in the country.'

The immediate crisis diminished with the hope of 'peace in our time' and Hitler's assurance that he had 'no further territorial demands to make on Europe'. Despite this, evacuation plans were worked out in greater detail and gas masks were fitted and distributed.

In the midst of these distractions, attention quickly returned to school when it was announced that a panel of twelve LCC inspectors would be spending a week examining books and lessons for the major ten-year inspection. The school found this visit 'both stimulating and appreciative', and noted the many changes since the last inspection had taken place.

Successes of Old Girls, who had gone to university or college, were regularly held up as examples for those still struggling to attain such honours. And from time to time, Old Girls wrote about college life or their careers for the school magazine. Some gave talks to the fifth and sixth, and other career talks were occasionally given.

In the hope that peace had been secured, the school's crowded year carried on with talks, visits, drama and singing competitions, musical recitals and the staff play. But by March 1939 the world picture looked ominous once more. Even so, nothing could stop the annual gym competitions, which this year were judged by Miss Knott from James Allen's and Miss Parker from Haberdasher Aske's; while sports, tennis and rounders matches continued through the summer term as lighter relief from swatting for the inevitable School Certificate and end of term exams.

With the usual end of term hymn, *Lord dismiss us with thy blessing,* ringing in their ears, girls left St Martin's with an uncertain feeling, wondering what the long summer holiday would bring. In August, when Hitler signed a pact of friendship with Stalin, war became inevitable. Teachers were hurriedly recalled from holiday as momentous upheavals were about to descend on the life of the school.

4. War Years: 1939 - 1945

On a sunny Saturday morning, at the beginning of September, two hundred girls made their way, two by two, down Tulse Hill. Under one arm many girls carried a rolled up blanket, over one shoulder hung a gas mask and in one pocket was a packet of raisins as part of their emergency 'iron rations'.

Parents followed in cars with bags, 'haversacks' and more girls. At Tulse Hill Station, staff, luggage, girls and gas masks came together to board a train for an unknown destination. They left a London ringed with silver barrage balloons suspended like giant legless elephants, whose cables waited to ensnare the droves of enemy planes that were anxiously expected. Everyone had been packed and ready for the past few days, waiting to be told when a train had been allocated for 'LCC H88'. And now, on the day before war was officially declared, plans that had been carefully made for more than a year were put into action.

At 6 o'clock that morning the girls, neatly dressed in winter uniform, had assembled in the school hall. Labelled luggage stood in neat piles. More girls and parents arrived. Some brothers and sisters, struggling with their own bulging bags, clustered round so that families could stay together.

A list of 'minimal essentials' had been provided which stated that a jersey was preferable to a blazer as it could be slept in if necessary, and that a rug or blanket, torch, needle and cotton, book, wool and knitting needles or sewing, stamped post cards and a small amount of money should be included.

Parents helped and encouraged as the children were numbered, labelled and divided into groups of ten, each in the care of a member of staff. Pauline Dadd vividly recalled the scene as the whole party set off:

'It was unbelievable and impossible to realize what was happening. We looked at the wardens in the street, wearing their tin helmets, and at the mistresses wearing their arm-bands inscribed LCC H88, but they were all outwardly calm and the whole affair still seemed nothing more than a ridiculous game. . . We were greeted by cheers from two groups of parents and friends who were lining our "route" and waving little Union Jacks. Feeling a queer desire to laugh and cry, we waved to them until we were on the platform. Then came the train and with the excitement of explorers into the unknown we bundled in.'

For half an hour, they sat with 'all eyes glued to the window wondering where we were going'. Some girls started on their packed lunch, but hurriedly stowed it away as the train pulled into Leatherhead Station. Doors clanged open and girls and luggage spilled out on to the platform. The large party made its orderly way to a church hall, and billets were eventually allocated, although this was made more difficult because two other evacuated schools had arrived in Leatherhead the day before.

Jenny Russell (née Taylor) was only four and a half when two St Martin's evacuees, dressed in brown winter overcoats and brown berets, stood on her doorstep. One became homesick and soon returned to London, but the other immediately became a big sister to Jenny.

Doreen Palmer (née Parr) was thirteen when she was evacuated, and well remembered the experience:

'Luckily my best friend and I were placed together and we very soon found ourselves in a little house in Queen Anne's Gardens in Linden Road, where we were welcomed and shown to our bedroom. We shared a double bed and had a washstand and basin in the room as there was no bathroom and only an outside toilet. We used to have a weekly bath in an old tin bath put in the kitchen, filled with water heated on the boiler. Later, we had a very small bedroom each because we made too much noise talking and giggling when we were together!'

The day after they arrived, Doreen's form mistress arranged a game of rounders on the nearby recreation ground in Poplar Road. Two local boys, who had been standing on the edge of the field watching the game, helped make up the team. The girls and the two boys became firm friends, not knowing that one day Doreen and one of the boys would marry.

In the first week of evacuation, Doreen and five other St Martin's girls spent some afternoons in the large garden of the Titley family, sewing curtain rings to blackout curtains. While they sewed they were fed with cakes, scones and apple and pear windfalls. There was a tennis court in the garden, which the girls were able to use, and a beautiful playhouse. In a row of shops, almost opposite the Leatherhead Institute, was the family grocery shop where the girls were allowed to help. 'Sometimes actually serving customers, but mainly stocking shelves and making up orders,' remembered Doreen.

In the interval between arriving at Leatherhead and the beginning of term, Joan Liddell, the Head Girl, arranged squads of older girls to help at the local hospital or WVS and with ARP arrangements. So, even before the term began, girls were gradually absorbed into Leatherhead life.

During this time, the staff visited the houses of the girls in their group to meet the hostesses and iron out any problems on either side. In summing up those first days as evacuees, Miss Bannister wrote:

> 'We were most grateful for the kindness of Leatherhead not only in providing food on our arrival, but in helping the staff in every way to find accommodation. The next important business was to find a home for the school, and we were most fortunate in being able to acquire the use of premises at St John's School, where we share with the boys the use of their modern block of classrooms, including excellent science laboratories, playing fields and gymnasium. The Junior and Preparatory Department works in a spacious room in the Wesley Hall and we have also rented netball and tennis courts.'

Sharing the facilities meant that while the 250 St John's boys were engaged in sports and other activities in the afternoons, St Martin's girls used the laboratories and the new classroom block, built on three sides of a rectangle.

At 1.15 the girls queued up outside the building waiting for the boys to leave by another door. Then, as Freda Smith remembered:

> 'Miss Thomas went in and inspected the school and when she thought it was quite "safe", she waved from a window and we all went in.'

An assembly was taken at 1.20 each day in a wide corridor in the new classroom block, when Miss Bannister, or Miss Thomas the deputy head, stood on the stairs to see above the cluster of girls standing quietly before them.

After initial reorganisation the girls were able to use the school library, gym and playing fields, but always at times when the boys were elsewhere so there was little chance of meeting. 'The masters,' it was unkindly rumoured, 'were so old they probably wouldn't notice if there were girls in the classroom.'

Art and singing — sometimes simultaneously — were added to the curriculum with the use of the Wesley Hall in Church Road. And juniors occasionally used the Old Cottage Hospital building. Detailed timetables showing where classes should be for each lesson were worked out, but wherever the location, school continued as normally as it could. A combined upper third report explained the daily arrangement for their year:

> 'We are divided into two Forms, S and J, as there are thirty-three girls altogether, and we have a captain for each Form. The majority of lessons we have together, but we have a few separately. There are four periods of thirty-five minutes each; and afternoon ends at 3.50. The signal for changing lessons is given, not by an electric bell, but by a Sixth Form girl walking along the corridor tinkling a triangle.'

When Grace Weston wrote of her war years at Leatherhead she recalled:

> '. . . the constant struggle to work, in the afternoons in St John's, in the mornings in all sorts of odd places: in the room at the Leatherhead Institute, in the rooms above the Wesley Hall, and in the room kindly lent to us by Mrs Mills.'

Mrs Mills was an evacuee hostess who enabled small groups, or individual girls, to have the use of one of her rooms for extra coaching with a member of staff. The room was also made available during the holidays for games and 'tea parties', a kind concession which was gratefully acknowledged and was to last the whole time the girls were at Leatherhead.

All through the evacuation, Miss Richmond, the maths teacher, made sure each girl had the regulation third of a pint of milk at a halfpenny a bottle. On icy days frozen cream protruded from each bottle forcing off its cap, so bottles were lined up on barely warm radiators to thaw out.

When some girls were able to work at St John's they walked back to the Wesley Hall for their milk, along Poplar Road where the delicious smell of new bread assailed them. At a farthing each, the baker sold crusts of bread which 'tasted gorgeous'. But usually the file of girls was accompanied by a prefect, so there could be no surreptitious eating in the street on those occasions.

At midday, girls again made their way through Leatherhead streets, this time to the Scout Hut where the hard-worked WVS cooked and served lunches for evacuees from many schools. The children sat close together at long trestle tables while Miss Ellis and her helpers worked in shifts to cope with the mountain of meals provided at 4d each. Later, when older girls were taking exams they were allowed to use the British Restaurant as it was less noisy.

With few buses, some girls cycled to school, others walked considerably further than they were used to, enjoying the freedom of the small country town. Bikes were parked in the boiler room, and coats and hats were laid out on desks in a spare room, before the girls hurried to their allocated classrooms. Old Johnian, Philip Morgan, said:

> 'The first sign of enemy occupation, as some would have it, was that certain objects appeared inside desks or lying on the floor . . . for instance hats and scarves, then there were pieces of knitting or delicate pieces of fabric which were presumed to be handkerchiefs.'

Those girls who did leave their hats at St John's, or who were caught wearing anything other than school uniform, could expect a severe reprimand from Miss Bannister.

As the girls often had to walk through the town, there were many occasions when the lack of correct uniform could be spotted. Yet, because of clothes rationing, acquiring it was always difficult. Freda Allen's mother had difficulty finding fawn ankle socks, and in desperation she dyed Freda's white socks with tea, so the regulation fawn could be worn.

The only exception to the rigid uniform rule was for evacuated girls who joined St Martin's from other schools. Judy Bird was one such girl, who came from Haberdasher Aske's, and was allowed to wear her original school uniform during her three years at Leatherhead.

Not all those at Leatherhead had been evacuated, for a group of girls travelled down by train each day from Tulse Hill or stations along the route. Yvonne McMillar (née Hirst) journeyed from Norbury and met up with the Head Boy of the Strand School, also travelling down to his evacuated school. But Yvonne did not realise then that she was talking to her future husband. As the war progressed, many girls who lived locally joined the school, most because it was now the nearest girls' grammar school, but some because it was a *London* grammar school with an excellent reputation.

At the start of term, form captains and prefects had been appointed as usual. Shorthand, typing and book-keeping, working towards the Royal Society of Arts examinations, were squeezed into the timetable by using a room in the Leatherhead Institute. But some subjects had to be dropped, as there was no time or space to fit them in. Freda Smith had taken Latin, chemistry and physics at Tulse Hill, and now found she had to choose between Latin and general science. Even so, despite these difficulties, a new routine was quickly established and accepted as 'normal'.

Back at Tulse Hill the school had closed down, with only Mr and Mrs Jones and Blake retained to look after the building. Mr Jones at once set to sand-bagging and reinforcing windows, ready for the expected bombing. He made an air raid shelter stretching over an area which had once been a small bicycle park, a store room and a connecting passage, and he fixed candle holders to the walls in case of electricity cuts. Being at the back of the old Silwood House this was the safest part of the building.

From time to time staff and sixth-formers returned from Leatherhead for books and equipment, reporting back on echoing footsteps along empty corridors, and a musty smell seeping through the disused building. Newspapers now covered books in the library,

St Martin's at Tulse Hill (Green)

and the domed roof of the inner entrance hall was completely blacked out.

By the end of 1939, when the expected raids hadn't materialised and the 'phoney war' continued, many children started drifting back to London. Girls who had not been evacuated, and those who returned, needed a school to go to. Anxious parents consulted the school, while Miss Bannister, staff and governors had meetings with the education authorities. After much discussion it was agreed that the school at Tulse Hill should re-open in January 1940 for morning classes only.

On that cold January morning girls started arriving early, waiting patiently by the top netball court for the back door to open. Islay Charman, the new Head Girl at Leatherhead, described the scene:

'The school was to open at 10 o'clock, but by 9.30 there was a considerable number of girls outside the back door. It was opened and they poured in. Only the lower cloakroom was to be used and after depositing hats, coats and shoebags, they charged up the stairs to the lower corridor (the upper one was not in use). Here more surprises awaited them; not only had parallel forms been united but the numbers were so small compared with our usual 400 that LV and UIV were to share a form room and similarly LIV and UIII.'

Parents with more girls, in a profusion of different uniforms, waited in the front entrance. Finally, an initial fifty girls were arranged into classes. But numbers rapidly multiplied in the first week and continued to increase as the weeks and months went by. Miss Bannister later reported:

'The framing of a time-table was a most interesting piece of school organisation, for the essential basis of the scheme was the possibility of running the school in two sections — in Leatherhead and in Tulse Hill with the same staff.'

Miss Thomas acted as head at Leatherhead, while Miss Bannister, having set the school on a firm evacuation footing, returned to Tulse Hill.

Some staff worked entirely at either Leatherhead or Tulse Hill, while others travelled between the two centres to keep some continuity of parallel education. The pre-war assistant cook had been re-engaged to help Mrs Jones, and later in the year a school cleaner and a kitchen helper were needed.

As the number of girls gradually increased, in May St Martin's at Tulse Hill was recognised by the LCC as a centre for tutorial classes. Now, girls not evacuated with their own school could be officially admitted. To begin with, classes went from the juniors up to the lower fifth, which meant that School Certificate exams were only taken at Leatherhead, where there were upper fifth and sixth form classes. In order to take their exams, those girls who still lived in London travelled by train each day to join the Leatherhead lessons.

One of the 'train girls', Josephine Williams (née Brown), remembered later in the year when she was waiting on the platform with a group of girls:

'There was a sudden noise of crackling and someone shouted, "Take cover!". Most of us dived back into the tunnel, but Yvonne took the first door behind her — two seconds later she came out blushing with embarrassment: she had entered the men's toilet and clearly rather than stay there preferred to face the German airman who was strafing the railway line before crossing the Channel.'

With the start of the blitz on London, in September 1940, school life at Tulse Hill became more uncertain. Waves of German aircraft bombed London each evening, setting the docks on fire which created a beacon of light that acted as a marker for further bombing raids. Most air raids lasted beyond midnight, so schools started an hour late to make up for disturbed nights. But because some girls at Tulse Hill were taken to school by their fathers, on the way to work, voluntary gym classes were started for a mixed age range from transition to lower fifth. Once a week, a voluntary discussion group for the upper fourths and lower fifths took place. Another morning the hall rang with singing as the choir practised.

Night raids were followed by daytime attacks, when 'dog fights' could be seen high in the sky as Spitfires and Hurricanes engaged the enemy planes. At the sound of the often-heard siren, girls hurried in orderly lines to the Silwood shelter, now housing benches around the walls of the cramped space. Here they continued their lessons when they could.

When a gym class was interrupted they studied first aid, and in science lessons experiments were carried to the shelter on trays. But sometimes science was marred by gas failure or a mere trickle of water coming from the taps. In November, a bomb that landed in the road just outside the school completely cut off gas and water supplies, creating a few days' holiday.

Although German aircraft were mostly heading for London, and Leatherhead wasn't a target, the golf course club house received a direct hit. Enemy planes overhead also meant danger because sometimes incendiary bombs were jettisoned as raiders made for home. So the long, wavering warning sound had become part of life at Leatherhead, too. Occasionally lessons were held in the wide lower corridor, where girls sat on the stone floor on coats or cushions. Pat Coe (née Denning) remembered her class being taken down to the boys' changing room area:

> 'After a while we were bored, so we started taking one garment from one locker and putting it in another. . . The boys must have been livid when they found out.'

But this was an isolated incident and generally girls carried on with lessons in the shelter area, or sat quietly waiting until the 'all clear' sounded.

Any girls who were going to another venue for their lessons had to ask local residents to take them in, either to shelter under the stairs or crowd into an 'Anderson' in the garden. Taylor's, a large shop in the centre of Leatherhead, opened up its basement, and the Old Cottage Hospital had an Anderson shelter in the grounds.

One focus for Luftwaffe attention was the Vickers aircraft factory at Weybridge, but despite air raid warnings and planes overhead, the greater danger was in London. Evacuees wondered how their families were coping when they heard reports of the third phase of the Battle of Britain, the relentless bombing raids on London. These continued until the end of the year, culminating in a massive incendiary raid on the capital.

Because schooling at Tulse Hill had been seriously disrupted throughout the autumn term, a week's voluntary school was held before the 1941 spring term. And after half-term, classes became full-time once more. Negotiating bomb craters and holes gouged in the pavements by incendiaries that had fallen all round the school, became an everyday occurrence. During the Easter holidays several incendiaries landed in the grounds and one went through the art room roof. Fortunately little damage was caused and school soon returned to wartime normal.

The only damage to St John's had been in March, when blast from a land mine, that fell on St Andrew's Convent half a mile away, flattened the gym. After that, gym classes were held in the vast assembly hall, where girls stripped off their tunics, leaving them in a heap, while they exercised in blouse and knickers as before.

As part of the Dig for Victory campaign, when parks, gardens and common land were dug up to grow vegetables, flower beds at Tulse Hill now grew lettuces, cabbage and potatoes. Girls also worked hard caring for a small vegetable plot, which Mr Jones had prepared by the side of the school pavilion. But the field became 'out of bounds' when an unexploded bomb sank into the clay. The long, uncut grass was later used for hay, so desperate was the need for Britain to be self-reliant. One enthusiastic fifth-former proudly said:

> 'I am doing my bit. I've got eight flower pots on my bedroom window sill. The family may laugh at me, but just wait until I can have a dinner consisting of my own home-grown vegetables!'

Leatherhead girls grew vegetables, too, after an allotment was made on a patch of waste land behind the canteen.

Staff and girls cleared away innumerable stones from a once-flourishing rockery, rambling roses had to be cut back and stinging nettles removed before planting could begin. Seeds were sown, with two girls attending each carefully labelled row. Watering and weeding continued through the year as successive crops of lettuce, peas, carrots and potatoes were harvested. By selling the produce to the canteen, evacuee hostesses and all who would buy it, essential money was raised for seeds and tools.

At the start of evacuation many school activities had been dropped, including the societies, but soon other interests took their place. A gardening club developed, and one morning each week a small discussion group was set up in Mrs Mills' room. Girls in the upper fifth and sixth forms studied home nursing and first aid, organised by the Leatherhead First Aid Post. Younger girls also attended the lectures and practical sessions, but they were not able to take the Red Cross exams which enabled older girls to become members of the Voluntary Aid Detachment (VADs).

There had been much to get used to with the new routine at Leatherhead, not just the school being housed in many buildings, which often meant long treks either walking or cycling between lessons. Settling in with a new family could cause problems, too, although most girls were able to help their host family in many ways by shopping, dog walking, baby minding, helping in the house, cooking and sometimes more help was needed when family members were ill.

In return, families took their charges to the cinema in Epsom or Dorking, or on shopping trips, picnics, outings and walks. Where there were girls of a similar age to the St Martin's evacuee, life-long friendships often resulted. Looking back, Ann Walker tells how she and her evacuee, Joan Newman, were like sisters, and that because of clothes rationing Ann's mother made clothes for both girls. Ruth Smith and her parents lived near St John's and at different times had four evacuees. Ruth went to Dorking Grammar School but there was no intense rivalry between the two schools.

Ten-year-old Gina Harrison joined the Upward family and became a younger sister to thirteen-year-old Betty, who was very excited when she heard 'a friend' was coming to stay. Gina helped with Betty's two-year-old sister, Sylvia, and when baby Joyce was born Gina's mother, who frequently visited, became Godmother to the new baby. During air raids the family slept downstairs in their steel, table-top Morrison shelter, which doubled as a table tennis table on other occasions.

The two older girls played with other children in the street or in nearby woods, and sometimes Mr Upward cycled with Betty and Gina so they could go further afield.

Some girls had season tickets for the tennis and swimming club, where they met up with young people from Leatherhead and other evacuated schools. Yet, talking to boys in the street was expressly forbidden for St Martin's girls, even though some of the boys were from 'evacuee families'. Instead, they sometimes met at the recreation ground. The girls were not supposed to fraternise with boys from St John's either, although as the majority were boarders there were fewer opportunities.

The Fetcham Village Hall Youth Club also attracted older girls from St Martin's, where they met local boys and girls, and boys from the Strand School which was evacuated to nearby Effingham.

Despite the war there were more occasions to socialise, with far greater freedom than there would have been in London. One favourite activity was to gather at The Splash at the end of River Road, Fetcham. In winter, hoards of children, both local and evacuated, skated and slid over the frozen water. In summertime boys dived off the bridge by the old lock gates, which were later blown away by a bomb and not replaced.

In contrasting her immediate feelings on being evacuated with those that developed later, M. Hillier in the upper fourth wrote:

> 'The days were dull in October. When I first came to Leatherhead the evenings were gradually getting darker and the leaves falling from the trees made the evenings seem dismal, and one ached for home and dear old noisy London. I got used to the school in St John's, and later things did not appear to be as bad as I first thought. On my new bicycle I gradually became familiar with the surrounding countryside and enjoyed short rides in the crisp, cold mornings which followed. Then came the fogs — a time which nobody enjoys — and the evenings seemed drearier than before. . . Cold set in and every night there was a frost. . . The bad frost over, the cold and snow continued, and it was difficult to get up in the morning. Then the weather began to change. . . trees came into leaf and small flowers began to appear in the hedgerows. The evenings became lighter and the sun lasted longer each day . . . Every day there are fresh signs of life and I wonder, now, if there can be a girl who aches for dusty, grimy London amidst the beauty of the country.'

During the first evacuation year sports matches had been inter-form. Tennis in the summer term, and netball in the autumn and spring, were played on courts hired from the Congregational Church or West Wing, the sports centre near the bus garage in Fetcham Grove. Fifth and sixth forms were also able to use grass courts at the Leatherhead Institute. Although inter-schools activities between St Martin's and St John's were not thought appropriate, Miss Jones, the French teacher, eventually managed to arrange a tennis match for the two schools. Freda Smith, remembering the occasion, wrote:

> 'However, no spectators were allowed. We couldn't decide whether Miss Bannister was more worried about the effect on her pupils or if St John's principal was more worried about his boys being contaminated by us!'

There was tennis in the summer term at Tulse Hill, too, with much practice in dinner hours and after school. And badminton, once an exclusive sport for the sixth form, was played by the lower fifth, now the most senior class at Tulse Hill.

Through an outbreak of German measles, no inter-schools hockey matches (girls only) could be played during the Autumn at Leatherhead — usually on one of St John's rugby pitches. And because of daylight raids, no games were allowed at Tulse Hill until after half-term of the spring term in 1941. Later that year, due to the unexploded bomb on the field, only netball and tennis could be played.

Because of restricted space at Leatherhead, drama by the whole school was no longer possible. Instead, individual class plays were rehearsed and acted to other classes and occasionally to a select audience. In the summer term, the upper fifth performed *Of Mice and Men* in the Wesley Hall, and the proceeds were jointly divided between the Red Cross and the Leatherhead Spitfire Fund. Sixth-former Grace Weston, in praising the performance, wrote:

> 'The Upper Fifth are to be congratulated on their enterprise in undertaking this production in the term in which they took their General School Examination. A good deal of hard work must have contributed to the result, for even the smallest parts were acted with spirit, while the parts of the heroine, the housekeeper, and the beadle (who subsequently became the dancing master) were especially well portrayed.'

But Josephine Williams, the heroine and producer, recalled that as a result of staging a 'public play' her class was banned from the dramatic competition that year.

A new, exciting experience for the girls at Leatherhead was to watch St John's school plays. Patricia Coe remembered word going round that there would be a 'silver collection' in the interval, so girls had hurried to the local post office to change their money. As they stood outside the school waiting to file into the main hall to watch *1066 and All That*, they clutched their silver threepenny bits — the smallest silver coin.

In the autumn, inter-schools hockey matches were arranged once more. Leatherhead played Dorking County School and nurses from the Blind School Hospital, while Tulse Hill played James Allen's. Entry into the Sutton Tournament was the first opportunity for both parts of St Martin's to be represented, when games were played at Sutton High School between several schools.

By 'entertaining the girls to tea in the Green Domino Café', seniors at Leatherhead returned a little of the hospitality they received after matches with Rosebery County at Epsom, Parson's Mead School and University College. The Green Domino Café, next door to West Wing, was again crowded with laughing, chattering schoolgirls after the upper fourth at Leatherhead had challenged the upper fourth at Tulse Hill to a netball match.

Rounders was another popular game, and matches were played with neighbouring Parson's Mead and Rosebery County schools. At first St Martin's team members missed the regular lunch hour practices they were used to before the war. Even so, matches and lessons were much enjoyed as a report indicated:

> 'We played rounders on St John's field — a beautiful field which is so well drained that even after rain it is usually possible to play on it, so that practices were very regular and the standard of play benefited greatly. . . Voluntary swimming was organised for some mornings and some after-school sessions. The open-air swimming pool at West Wing was the scene of activity and swimmers gathered there in their free time.'

St John's playing field (St John's School)

Using free time, particularly in holidays and at weekends, could have been a problem for evacuees, because children were not encouraged to return to London. But loneliness and feeling homesick were kept to a minimum as many activities were arranged. Vera le Voi, of the lower fourth, described one of her interests:

> 'My Saturday mornings in Ashtead are very enjoyable and I look forward to them with eagerness. About six months ago the Parson's Mead girls invited the St Martin's girls to join their Guide meetings. Five of us. . . were happy to do so. . . We arrive at 9.30 at Parson's Mead School and begin the morning with a Bible reading read by a different Patrol Leader each week. . . If the weather permits we garden. Each Patrol has a separate piece of ground for growing vegetables. . . At other times we have very interesting games, when we are not doing Guide work or passing tests. We score points for the games, and there is a cup awarded for the best Patrol. As soon as the weather turns warmer we are hoping to have a hike, and are going to cook some of our food by a camp fire. When the weather is not suitable for outdoor games we have country dancing.'

In good weather there was much exploring to be done around the small town, with its 'narrow pavements, little shops and quaint eighteenth century cottages'. Enid Treispeuh, in the upper fourth, described the neighbouring countryside:

> 'Further from the town are fields and copses, with funny little paths running through them, and the place on the bank of the river where small boys go tiddling. There are steep hills, which are worth climbing just to see the view; the sun which sets red in a background of purple clouds and bright blue sky; small yet sweet-smelling wild flowers; tall and majestic trees; songs of the many birds; the noise and clatter of a busy street.'

And an anonymous evacuee commented:

> 'Town lovers are not always country lovers, and here, too, we have had to adapt ourselves and what at first seemed a very long way with no trains and only infrequent or no buses now has become a very pleasant daily walk. There are but few cinemas and shops, but we have discovered excellent substitutes in many good walks and cycle rides.'

Despite school holidays being shortened because of the war, there was much time to fill. As well as the many activities suggested by hostesses, St Martin's staff arranged a regular rota for keeping the girls occupied. Patricia Rees, in the lower sixth, showed how it was organised:

'It was necessary to report at Wesley Hall each morning, and there we discussed the programme for the day. All suggestions were carefully considered. Although activities were planned with care, it was not compulsory to take part in them if other arrangements had been made with our hostesses. Plans for our amusement varied from gardening to giving impromptu concerts. . . Charades, songs, poems and musical interludes, not forgetting the buns and cakes supplied most kindly by the mistress in charge, contributed to a very enjoyable morning.'

Tennis, walking, climbing Box Hill and Mickleham Downs, and keep fit classes which followed the wireless programme *Up in the Morning Early*, all enabled holidays to pass happily. Old Girl, Pat Coe, felt that because of living in Surrey they had more freedom 'cycling, walking over to Dorking, blackberry picking and making our own entertainment'. And there was always knitting.

Knitters all over the country were kept busy making balaclavas, scarves, jerseys, gloves and socks. Schools were encouraged to contribute, for even the poorest knitters could make squares for blankets. Wool was supplied by the WVS and often this was unravelled from old jerseys. An appeal for knitted garments for the Royal Engineers and their prisoners of war was taken up by the girls and staff at Leatherhead. Miss Copland alone made twenty pairs of socks, and was always seen with knitting at hand.

One activity which continued throughout the war, both at Leatherhead and Tulse Hill, was the Charities Fund. Margaret Wells, a sixth-former, explained the work of the fund:

'The money is collected by the girls not only in collections once a week, but also from school plays and other activities from which a proportion of the proceeds goes to the Charities Fund. There are certain charities to which we subscribe annually: the Great Ormond Street Children's Hospital, the Rev. Pat McCormick's Christmas Fund, and our own Allen Loan Fund. We also help the Ranyard Mission, but in this case we send clothes, many of which the girls make themselves.

'It was decided that we should send £5.5s. to the Red Cross Fund towards the cost of an ambulance which is being subscribed for by schools in the British Isles. £2.2s. is to be sent to the Life Boat Fund, and we have already sent £1.4s. to the Save the Children Fund.'

Besides these ongoing collections, there were special national *weeks*, such as 'war savings', 'tanks' and 'warships', when money was raised by a variety of concerts, competitions, raffles, sales and the popular 'farthing collection'. A Comforts Fund for the sailors of HMS *Scout* also received a generous donation, as HMS *Scout* had been 'adopted' by the people of Leatherhead. Books were collected to send to the British Seamen's Society, and these were distributed amongst merchant seamen.

Even though money had to be stretched in many directions, regular weekly collections for National Savings in the first two years raised £1,961.16s. at Leatherhead and £1,422. 10s. 6d at Tulse Hill. Nationwide, most people responded to the desperate need for money and goods, and St Martin's played an active part.

Another way in which everyone helped was by saving salvage. Aluminium, glass, rubber and paper, as well as pig food, were diligently saved. Bones were collected to make cordite for cartridges, and metal of all kinds was urgently needed. Paper was so scarce that one term's school reports were written on the reverse of the preceding term's — and one girl commented:

> 'Much paper and mental anguish could be saved by the total abolition of these documents!'

One item which was keenly collected was shrapnel, gathered up after each air raid:

> 'We were up very early in the morning,' remembered Phyllis Holmes (née Matchin), 'and the roads would be alive with children collecting shrapnel and shell caps. It did, in fact, get earlier every morning or someone else would get the best pieces.'

Evelyn Westcott, in the upper sixth, reported:

> 'A shrapnel collection was started and at least 400lbs have been salvaged to date; everyone has helped and the innumerable tiny bits were not despised, although the larger "show" specimens were welcome and duly inspected.'

Through all these extra activities the curriculum continued as best it could, and a time for homework in the mornings had now been arranged, as Pamela Horder in the upper fourth described:

'The Prep Room is in St John's Library, where we can sit and do our prep every day excluding the weekend, from 10 o'clock to 12.15. There are tables where we are privileged to be able to use ink, because the boys are not allowed to do so. There is a mistress in charge, and we are not allowed to talk. In the very hot weather it is extremely cool, and we can work in comfort. Sometimes there are lessons going on at the far end of the room, but this is not disturbing because the room is so large.'

Problems were gradually being ironed out and a wartime routine firmly established.

With much reduced fifth and sixth forms, twenty-one girls passed their School Certificate. Fifteen gained Matric and fourteen of these were awarded LCC Intermediate County Scholarships. Miss Bannister reported:

'Our School Certificate results last year were definitely good, especially considering the changed conditions under which the school is working; and we congratulate our Head Girl, Daphne Reynolds, on winning an Open Exhibition of £20 a year to St Hugh's College, Oxford.'

Despite the much interrupted and fragmented timetable, the number of girls taking Higher School Certificate remained constant, and several girls went on to university.

One Saturday, towards the end of the autumn term, having watched St John's performance of *Bulldog Drummond* in the morning, the 'voluntary singing group', with Miss Copland and her small dulcitone, made their way to the new Leatherhead Cottage Hospital to sing carols to the patients. Sixth-former Kathleen Collins described their visit:

'The Matron greeted us and told us that we were to sing in each of the three main wards. As she took us along to the first ward, we were very much impressed by the beautiful new hospital. . . We sang quietly at first, as it was strange to sing to people lying in bed, and the dulcietone sounded so different from a piano. But we soon became accustomed to these things and sang heartily and with enjoyment.'

Miss Copland was always anxious that good music should be heard, particularly now that she was unable to play her soothing selection before Prayers. Instead she arranged 'Musical Chats'. Early in the spring term of 1942, with snow still covering the ground, Miss Copland took the theme of 'seasons' for her 'chat' in the Wesley

Hall. In an earlier musical chat, themed 'children in music', Miss Copland tactfully showed through selected pieces how children of different nationalities had much in common with each other.

On the corner of Church Street and Poplar Road stood an old house where the Leatherhead School of Music held regular choir practices. Doreen Palmer remembered how she and several of her friends 'had the audacity to join the choir'. They had no voice test and she felt 'it said a lot for the older members of the choir that they put up with us'. They practised *The Messiah*, until the novelty wore off and the girls moved elsewhere for entertainment.

One major event that permeated the life of the school was Miss Bannister's retirement. Miss Bannister had seen St Martin's through many changes, but the time came at the end of the spring term when she travelled down to Leatherhead to take her last assembly, in the library at St John's. The Head Girl, Brenda Woodward, presented Miss Bannister with a rug and reading lamp from the girls, in gratitude for all her work. Earlier, at a staff party held at St Ermin's, Westminster, the staff had presented their gifts.

Vice-chairman of the governors, Mr W.F. Marchant, wrote in the school magazine of the many formidable problems Miss Bannister had had to overcome in her all but thirty years as headmistress. He particularly stressed:

> 'Her greatest triumph was no doubt the successful opening, in spite of very great hindrance, of the classes at St Martin's in January 1940, which enabled most of the girls who did not go with the school to Leatherhead to get back to work with the loss of only one term's schooling, perhaps a record for London. . . I wonder how many of the girls have known that from the beginning of the war, except for the first short period when she was billeted in Leatherhead, Miss Bannister was "in residence" in St Martin's school building, none too comfortable a billet, and that she organised and herself took part in the nightly air raid watch, giving active help in the preservation of the building on the night when an incendiary bomb pierced the roof and many others fell in the grounds.'

As an entertainment for Miss Bannister, the juniors put on a performance of the play they had previously only shown to parents, hostesses and the upper third. Second former Brenda Belcher recalled it with pride:

'We "The Juniors" acted a play called *The Wizard of Oz*. We collected £2 for Mrs Churchill's "Aid to Russia Fund". After the play we had songs and recitations. The Producer did everything herself; we had no help from Miss Miles, except that she lent us her fur coat for the lion. . . We acted the play on the last day of term also, because Miss Bannister was leaving. All the school came to see it and we had a jolly time.'

Unlike many of her predecessors, Miss Bannister was fortunate in her active retirement, for apart from a continued interest in the school she involved herself with the Westminster Company of the Girls' Training Corps, which prepared girls for life in the services.

Many were the tributes to her, including those of the new headmistress, Miss Kathleen Gordon Ewen, who had taught history at Charing Cross. When the school moved to Tulse Hill Miss Gordon Ewen became joint Housemistress of St Martin's House, with Miss Thomas, both of whom became vice-presidents of the school's Historical Society which formed soon after the move. In 1935 Miss Gordon Ewen had left the school to become Senior History Specialist at James Allen Girls' School in Dulwich, and in 1938 she became headmistress of Guildford High School. But now, in the midst of war, St Martin's welcomed her back.

Miss Gordon Ewen's regal and somewhat awe-inspiring appearance was always countered by an engaging, twinkling smile that readily put even the most apprehensive offender at ease. At her first assembly, Miss Gordon Ewen reminded the school that Miss Bannister and her predecessors had established a great tradition. 'It is up to us to carry it on,' she said.

St Martin's settled down once more as it weathered another change. But this change appeared seamless because traditions, routine and the smooth running of the school remained the same in its two locations. Miss Gordon Ewen was based at Leatherhead and visited Tulse Hill twice a week, where Miss Thomas was acting head.

One of Miss Gordon Ewen's first duties was to record the death of Miss Humphry, who had been chairman of the governors when the school moved to Tulse Hill, and an active member of the governing body both at Charing Cross and Tulse Hill. Her father, as vicar of St Martin-in-the-Fields, had been chairman before her. In her first

School Notes for the magazine, Miss Gordon Ewen wrote:

> 'Since 1870 her family has been connected with the school and we have been indebted to Miss Humphry for much information about the history of the school.'

To honour the Humphry family's long association with the school, the Humphry Essay Prize had been endowed by Mrs Grace Western, niece of Miss Humphry.

Each year, books to the value of two pounds were divided between the writers of the best historical essays. Subjects were varied, and in 1942 the chosen topic was 'The Diary of an Elizabethan from 1584-1596'. Mrs Western and Sir Edward Midwinter, Chairman of the Governors, carefully appraised each essay.

For over two years, young Canadian soldiers had been billeted in Leatherhead. Some with great expertise had built a bailey bridge over the River Mole, so that tanks and armoured vehicles arriving for repairs could avoid the narrow streets in the town. Doreen Palmer remembered the day a party of girls took a picnic and walked along the river bank towards Mickleham. They stopped to talk to a group of Canadian soldiers, then happily accepted a lift, clambering on to their huge tank to be swayed and jolted as it rumbled along the road. On 'flag days', when Doreen and her friends collected in the town, they always found the Canadians 'most generous in their giving'.

The shortage of teachers at that time was made more apparent when Mrs Davies, from the Preparatory Department, was 'lent to a boys' school for the time being'. Miss Harris, another St Martin's teacher, divided her day with St John's, and many of their masters had come out of retirement to help the war effort, because of the shortage of teachers.

National Savings, money-raising events and salvage collections continued. The privations of rationing carried on, and eking out a meagre sweet ration was particularly felt, although for many children unrationed Ovaltine and Horlicks tablets became good substitutes. Doreen Palmer missed the Tuck Shop provided by Blake at Tulse Hill before the war, so she and her friends used to:

'. . .bombard Mr Tutt in his sweet shop in Bridge Street on the way to West Wing, and plead with him for any sweets off-ration.'

Margaret Jones didn't forget a special occasion when the American Red Cross sent a consignment of boiled sweets to augment the sweet ration:

'They were different shapes and colours from our boiled sweets,' Margaret commented, 'and I was not very fond of sweets in general, but I felt very grateful to the Americans for their generosity.'

One way of counteracting the effects of the war, for older girls, was by going to Harvest Camp. In 1943, both halves of the school came together to work on the land at Crudwell near Malmesbury in Wiltshire. Miss Sutton and Miss Jones, both dressed in 'business-like dungarees', greeted the party and showed them to the large barn which was to house them throughout their stay. Hard work, hunger and humour all played their part. In describing one incident, Joy Allingham, in the upper fifth, wrote:

'After five minutes hard walking through the mangolds, past cows and into the farmyard, we saw Miss Sutton's car. Two orderlies staggered towards us carrying dixies, filled with something which smelt delicious. They were followed by a motley crew consisting of ducks and chickens, who evidently could smell just as well as we could. There were sighs of satisfaction as we sank into the straw and helped ourselves to fishcakes — hot out of the oven. One particularly ugly hen stalked up to me, seized my fishcake and fluttered off, without so much as a "thank you"! I had to appease my hunger with rock cakes and apples, but I consoled myself with the thought that there was a whole field of mangolds awaiting my return.'

Maisie James, also from the upper fifth, summed up her feelings:

'Many memories come crowding back at the thought of Harvest Camp. Dashing for first place in the wash-house in the chilly mornings; watching one's first load of hay go swaying to the rick, threatening to fall off at any moment; looking over the ancient abbey at Malmesbury. But most of all we remember the kindness of the people of Crudwell, and how welcome they made us.'

When the girls climbed back into the lorry and were driving off, they felt as if they were leaving friends and surroundings they had known for much longer than three weeks.

Back at school, strict discipline continued to be enforced and Jean Walton recalled the solemn occasion when they were summoned to the hall by Miss Thomas. A St Martin's girl had been to the bakers' shop at the bottom of Tulse Hill to buy buns, and had been reported because she had forgotten to say thank you. There was a shocked silence, and Miss Thomas impressed on the older girls the need to watch over the younger ones to make sure their manners were always impeccable.

Eating buns in the street was definitely not allowed, at Tulse Hill or Leatherhead, as Daphne Barton (née Wood) remembered:

> 'Once a group of us were reported for being seen eating buns in the town. We were summoned to the headmistress and were really told off about letting down the standard of the school. We thought we might be expelled.'

Fraternising with boys remained a forbidden pastime, too, but some girls at Leatherhead devised a way of leaving notes for boys, hidden in an old house in The Crescent. 'It was all rather tame,' said Daphne Barton, 'and eventually someone reported us, so after another telling off it stopped.' More notes were left in desks for boys to find, and Philip Morgan remembered that his friend, Hugh Silk, exchanged notes with Yvonne Taverne, who used his desk in the afternoon:

> 'Hugh was always unwilling to reveal exactly what went on,' he said, 'or even whether they ever met, but Hugh's prestige, always high, soared to unprecedented heights. Other boys claimed minor conquests but nobody believed them and such exploits were merely nine days wonders.'

But sometimes meetings with boys were quite unexpected.

When a group of girls was being marched from one part of the school building to another, suddenly a group of boys came running from their showers, with only towels round them. Red faced with confusion the poor mistress commanded, 'Look the other way, girls!' as she tried to hurry on her giggling group.

Occasional air raid warnings continued to disrupt the day, and if a siren sounded during lunch time everyone made for the nearest shelter. Jenny Taylor, who by now had joined her evacuee at St Martin's, hurried from the Scout Hut to her house nearby, to sit under the huge dining room table with her friends — where they continued to eat the plates of lunch they had brought with them.

One day Joan Church (née Osborn) watched the twisting, turning vapour trails of a 'dog fight' high up in the sky. As she watched, a pilot floated down on his parachute. On another occasion, Joan and three friends were being driven out of Leatherhead in an open-topped car when a German plane suddenly swooped down, machine gunning the road. Driver and girls leapt from the car and scuttled into a ditch until the plane had gone by.

Successive years added more girls and a new class to the top of the school at Tulse Hill, so more teachers were needed. But there was still an acute shortage, even with some staff working at both halves of the school by splitting their day. Although this sometimes left a gap at Leatherhead, it was readily filled by prefects teaching younger girls. Jenny Russell remembers her evacuee, Yvonne Fenton, teaching her English and reading *Black Beauty* to the class housed in the Old Cottage Hospital. Another prefect taught geography, while others helped with games. This proved to be valuable teaching practice which later helped girls who went on to teacher training colleges.

The School Council, temporarily suspended because of the war, was reconvened which led to clubs and societies starting again. At Tulse Hill, the Dramatic Club re-formed, a current affairs club was started and at the first meeting of the Music Club nearly seventy girls heard Miss Copland discuss the life of Handel, with musical examples. Leatherhead started a film club and members were given sound advice from a film critic on how to criticise constructively, including the direction, actors and use of music.

The Old Girls Association (OGA) continued throughout the war with its twice yearly meetings. But wartime conditions were evident by a notice in the magazine which said, 'Tea will be provided, but please bring your own buns.'

Citizenship now became a major concern of the school, and Aileen Daw (lower sixth) wrote:

'We must prepare ourselves for all that lies ahead, for this is the important task that all the youth of the world has to undertake.'

parts of the building, and we are already well accustomed to the noise of the builders who will be with us for some time.'

The Preparatory Department temporarily squashed round a large table at the back of Trinity Rise Church. Here, as a break from reading and writing practice, there were general knowledge and multiplication table quizzes. But lessons were makeshift and did not last long, so the juniors stayed at home for the summer term.

Despite bomb damage temporarily closing the Senior School, the restrictions this imposed and the reduced number of girls, Salute the Soldier Week achieved amazing results at Tulse Hill and Leatherhead. Both sections doubled their projected money-raising targets, with the sums of £2,106.10s and £1,102.17s 6d collected at the two locations. This boosted the amount so far raised by the school for the 'war effort' to a staggering £11,710. When compared with average earnings of under five pounds a week, and a loaf of bread costing fourpence halfpenny (about 2p), these were remarkable results. But as Miss Dunnicliff said, 'there was a burnt-out top floor to avenge.'

Just after the uplifting news of the allied D-Day landings in France, on the 6th of June, another blow literally fell, when a strange sight was seen over Southern England. The strange sight was a V1 — *Vergeltungswaffe* — pilotless aircraft, which became known as the flying bomb or *doodlebug*. Although their target was central London, most fell short so that south of the Thames received much of the onslaught that followed.

One morning as Jean Hey cycled up Tulse Hill, a doodlebug flew overhead. When Jean arrived at school and said she had kept on cycling, Miss Thomas, in her gentle way, said, 'I lay flat in a front garden. Next time I want you to do the same.'

But St Martin's at Tulse Hill was again forced to close, and only girls taking their School Certificate examinations were allowed in school. Flying bombs had begun a week before the exams started, and because the examination papers had already been distributed postponement was not possible. Provision for taking the exams was hurriedly made in the Silwood shelter.

Raids day and night meant loss of sleep, houses damaged and last minute revision in Anderson shelters or under the stairs. But for a small group of girls the war became secondary. Doreen Brown recalled the never-to-be-forgotten week of her exams:

'On that fateful Friday morning, a little band of apprehensive Upper V-ites plodded up Tulse Hill, regardless of the Alert which was still on and only thinking of the horrors of the examination ahead of them. In twos and threes they gathered in the Silwood cloakroom and after hanging their tin-hats and coats on the pegs, began feverishly to look up last minute facts. . . Members of the staff who were to invigilate came down to see us, looking far too bright and cheery to our jaundiced gaze. Then Miss Jesson, our form mistress, appeared carrying a telegram which she read. "Best of luck, Up.V" and signed "From the Sixth".'

Leatherhead had not forgotten them, which cheered the little group as they filed into the shelter, where card tables and chairs were assembled. Doreen continued:

'Our feelings as Miss Thomas opened the blue packet and distributed those first question papers cannot be described, but after the first half hour our nerves gradually settled down and our self confidence began to reassert itself. . . During the middle of the morning, milk would be brought round to us and the silence would be disturbed by the munching of biscuits as well as the scratchings of pens and the sighs and coughs of examinees. We usually had our dinner in the Cookery Kitchen if there was no Alert on, but more often than not we ate it in the shelter with our plates precariously balanced on our knees.'

When there was no air raid alert, girls were allowed to walk round the gardens after lunch, but they quickly raced back to the shelter if a warning sounded. When an alert was in progress the girls stood on the driveway 'to get a breath of fresh air and clear our heads for the next examination', always ready to dive back to the shelter if a doodlebug was heard.

Despite the increase in flying bombs, girls' houses being damaged and an average of two or three warnings each morning, with barely half an hour between them, the exams carried on:

'Whenever a bomb came too near, the invigilator would cry "Duck!" and simultaneously nineteen candidates would roll off their chairs and try unsuccessfully to sandwich themselves under their tables. After the crash we would scramble to our feet grinning weakly at each other, then taking a sip of milk to fortify ourselves we would continue that fatal struggle with our memories!'

Thankfully for Doreen and her class:

'That seemingly interminable week dragged to its weary close, and after the last examination paper had been collected we joyfully stacked away our tables and nineteen weary but relieved schoolgirls hurried home.'

When the results finally came through, thirty-two girls from Tulse Hill and Leatherhead gained their School Certificate, nineteen with Matric. Of these, eleven gained LCC Intermediate County Scholarships, which they held over in the sixth form while they were 'preparing for definite careers'.

Although flying bombs were aimed at London, and believed to be landing on the capital, a proportion landed in Kent, Sussex and Surrey, so girls at Leatherhead were also affected. Daphne Barton remembered an occasion when:

'We were in the middle of an exam — about thirty of us in a large classroom at St John's with a lot of windows. Suddenly we heard an awful droning overhead. We looked round at each other, but no one said a word. Then the noise stopped. Instantly Miss Wheeler shouted, "Get under your desks." There was the worst bang I have ever heard and the whole building shook. Very calmly, Miss Wheeler told us to get up and walk to the door in a line, which we did, and she took us down the stairs and told us to sit quietly on the floor in the corridor without talking. About forty-five minutes later the All Clear went, and we were told to go back to the classroom, where we finished the exam. After school we found that the doodlebug had crashed into a field at the bottom of the town. Some sheep were killed and a lot of broken glass was about. Thinking back, I am full of admiration at the calmness of Miss Wheeler, our Latin teacher.'

Altogether sixteen flying bombs exploded in the Leatherhead area, and because of air raid warnings lessons were often interrupted.

Tennis matches were curtailed after early enthusiastic practice at West Wing and many matches had to be cancelled. A second Harvest Camp enabled older girls temporarily to escape the invasion of doodlebugs, and girls who had attended camp the previous year felt experienced enough to laugh at their mistakes.

Supersonic V2 rockets followed the onslaught of flying bombs, and disrupted life still further. Each devastating, catastrophic explosion came without warning, and with it a rising pall of black smoke was seen for miles around. But events abroad were moving swiftly, and despite V1s and V2s exploding, mainly in South London, talk of the war soon ending was raising hopes.

In September, St Martin's at Tulse Hill reopened once more. But now 'out of bounds' notices were placed on both flights of concrete stairs, preventing entry to the top floor. Books were water stained and some had blackened covers and edges; and a wet, burnt smell pervaded the building. At the end of the afternoon, if an air raid warning had sounded, no one was allowed home without written consent from parents. But a strange air of determination prevailed as staff and girls came to terms with the restrictions.

Each section of the school worked through the busy autumn term knowing the war could not drag on much longer. The highlight for girls at Tulse Hill was the end of term Christmas entertainment. After the lower third had acted scenes from *Little Women*, and the upper fourth performed a short French play, came the much-anticipated staff contribution of two Hilaire Belloc tales — *Albert and the Lion* and *Matilda*.

This happily rounded off a haphazard term when V1s and V2s still fell, though fewer in number. Through the spring term, signs of war ending became daily evident, so on the 8th of May 1945, when Victory in Europe (VE day) was declared, the relief was overwhelming. Yvonne Taverne in the upper sixth wrote:

'Although we were waiting for this news all the weekend, it still came as something unbelievable.'

A party of girls from Leatherhead went up to Piccadilly Circus where crowds surged forward in a mass of red, white and blue. 'In the brilliant sunshine, it looked as though everyone was dressed in uniform,' Yvonne said.

The two halves of the school remained separate for the summer term. But the start of the 1945 autumn term would not only see them reunited, but heralded further great changes in the school.

5. Together Again: 1945 - 49

At the end of the summer term, in 1945, the girls at Leatherhead packed up their belongings and said goodbye to St John's and Leatherhead's familiar places. With a mixture of feelings, they left the families where some had belonged for nearly six years. But sadness was allayed by a natural longing to see their own homes and families again, and promises were made to keep in touch, as many life-long friendships had been made.

'St Martin's girls have been very happy evacuees, thanks to the kindness of the people of Leatherhead,' said Miss Gordon Ewen, at a farewell gathering at the Leatherhead Institute. And she related how the WVS had brought lunch to the children when they couldn't get to the canteen because of raids. She paid tribute to the people who had acted as hostesses and who had shown 'most patient understanding'.

The Chairman of the Governors, Sir Edward Midwinter, thanked Mr Jack Carter the Headmaster, for 'making possible the use of premises at St John's'. To mark their appreciation, St Martin's later presented a plaque to the people of Leatherhead, which was placed in the Council Chamber of the old council building in Bull Hill.

Having *broken up*, the school at Leatherhead then *packed up*, and the following day the upper fifth and sixth, from both sections of the school, met at Tulse Hill to help the staff move in furniture, equipment and books, which were returning from Leatherhead. Maisie James described the scene:

> 'There was an expectant air among the girls who assembled in the front hall for this preparation, for the reunion of the school was an historic occasion. . . There was plenty of work to be done while waiting for the van loads to arrive, for the contents of cupboards had to be rearranged, shelves dusted, books transferred from classrooms to cellar and vice-versa. Soon the corridors resounded with the noise of footsteps and voices.'

Some girls would only know St Martin's at Leatherhead, having joined from local areas and left before the school could be reunited. One such girl, Betty Springall, summed up her thoughts, which epitomise feelings of schooldays wherever their location:

'My first day at St Martin's found me in a bright check dress and huge panama hat, walking up St John's drive. . . feeling a little apprehensive of meeting so many new people. . . In the months that followed, came the first end-of-term exams., the dramatic competition when I was a juryman in "Roast Pig", and then the pride with which I received my first gym stripe. . . I then moved up to LIV. . . and read my first Shakespeare play.

'I remember the feel of the first hockey stick in my hand and the vain attempt to hit the hard white ball. And so other school years ended, with the School Certificate on the as yet distant horizon. We went through upper IV and Lower V at last finding ourselves part of the senior school, voting with more consideration for our Form Captain and giving deeper thought to Founders' Day and world affairs. . . At long last we became Upper Vs. Now more subdued and finding School Certificate far too near, a matter of weeks. . . As the curtain falls and a new life begins, there are many memories to store away. . . I have seen Miss Bannister go and Miss Gordon Ewen come, and various Head Girls take up their position and then leave for university. . . I shall remember acting in a community, the hustle and bustle in the cloakroom after the last bell. . . the thought of work successfully done and, above all, the wild hilarious cheering at our breaking up.'

Other girls who had joined the school at Leatherhead would travel up to Tulse Hill by train each day, with time to catch up on unfinished homework — or spent chatting to boys from the Strand School or Dulwich College. Still more, who had left Tulse Hill as small girls, would be returning with responsibilities of seniors.

In September the whole school was 'safely gathered under one roof', although bomb damage meant 'out of bounds' notices remained on the concrete staircases, preventing access to the top floor. Scaffolding covered much of the building, and builders and their materials seemed to be everywhere.

Two head girls, ten prefects and fifteen vice-prefects were appointed to take on the added duties of the enlarged numbers, which were now divided into three streams for each senior year. Sadly for the school, two longstanding members of staff, who had stayed on until the war ended, now retired. Miss Freeth after thirty-three years and Miss Dunnicliff after thirty.

Miss Thomas stayed on for one more term to see the school back together at Tulse Hill. She retired at Christmas after thirty-two years as a mainstay of the school. Her loss was greatly felt, but Miss Thomas, like many staff in retirement, kept her interest in the school's activities and remained in close contact. Other staff had taken the opportunity to move on to new schools, and a fresh intake joined St Martin's. A new gardener and extra part-time cleaners were also engaged.

After Miss Thomas left, the position of deputy head changed to 'Second Mistress' and at first was given, in turn, to senior mistresses for one year.

On the 11th of November, at eleven o'clock, thanksgiving services were held all over the country. Three days later, because transport difficulties prevented the school from travelling up to Charing Cross, the vicar of St Martin-in-the-Fields, the Reverend Eric Loveday, joined Canon Edwards in conducting a service at nearby Holy Trinity Church in Trinity Rise. This was the first occasion when both sections of the school, with parents, friends and Old Girls, could be together after the long separation.

The war had pin-pointed many weaknesses in the education system, and it was intended that these should now be remedied by setting education 'in a framework of improved welfare and social justice'. Slowly, changes began to be made throughout the country, when free school milk and medical examinations became part of school life.

A school doctor, Dr Gillie, was appointed to St Martin's, and once a year girls in turn were called from their lessons to hurry down to the cloakrooms, where they stripped down to vest and brown school knickers. Chattering nervously they put on plimsolls and an overcoat or raincoat, then trailed up to the top of Silwood to be greeted by their mother. Now talking in subdued whispers, they waited to be called into the rest room for the medical inspection.

With the severe shortage of teachers, an emergency scheme for one-year teacher training courses was set in motion, some in specially created colleges. But most educational changes, suggested by the 1944 Education Act, were to wait for another two years.

Once the girls were back together, the high standard of discipline and courtesy in both sections of the school remained, and lateness was not tolerated without a good reason. If after hurrying to the cloakroom door it was found to be locked — promptly at 9 o'clock each morning — the late-arriver made her anxious way up the side path to the front entrance.

Here she would be admitted by Miss Smyth, the elderly school secretary of many years' standing, then told to sit on the bench outside Miss Gordon Ewen's room to wait and explain her lateness. Valerie Punter (née Nex) remembered the only time she was late was the morning her war-bride sister sailed for Canada:

> 'I was confronted by an irate Miss Smyth, but Miss Gordon Ewen, gazing at my tear-stained face, was kindness itself.'

Slowly the school picked up the threads of pre-war days, as societies and clubs that had lapsed re-emerged. The English Society's 126 members had an inter-form quiz on authors, titles and characters of well-known books. They discussed such topics as 'Which modern books will become classics?' and 'Can a married woman have a career?'

The Classical Society re-formed with fifty members studying Greek theatre. Later, by re-joining the Inter Schools Classical Club, a much enlarged membership enabled professional lecturers to talk on a wider range of subjects.

Sixty members of the Society of Modern Languages enjoyed a play acted by Miss Jones and Miss Warren, and took part in a discussion on the conditions in post-war France. The Science Club came into being again with a Brains Trust, and by borrowing a projector, members were able to see a film called *The Working of the Telephone*.

The Historical and Current Affairs Society continued with visits to newspaper offices, talks on the history of the Tower of London and scenes illustrating children through the ages. Members of the ever-popular Music Club heard the life stories of Chopin and Tchaikovsky, with musical examples played by Miss Copland and some of the members, or on gramophone records. Later still the Geographical Society was added to the list.

The Film Club, which had started in Leatherhead, heard the behind-the-scenes processes of film making. And after visiting the cinema to see *The Wicked Lady*, a 'heated discussion' took place. But heated discussions, visits and quizzes all helped unite the school once more.

Producing *Quality Street* was another activity which helped bring the school back to its former close-knit community. The play had once been produced in Charing Cross in the confines of the drill hall, but now a more elaborate production was envisaged when preliminary readings, then rehearsals, started in the autumn term. Two casts were chosen to alternate the final performances, and girls, parents and staff helped create convincing scenery.

Most of the cast had colds or 'flu at some time during the spring term, and some withdrew altogether because of the pressure of school work, but despite these set-backs time passed quickly. Authentic costumes were hired and last-minute alterations hurriedly made, as everyone eagerly awaited the production. Tickets were sold in advance for five performances, and afterwards a report in *The West Norwood Times* said:

'A fine performance of J.M. Barrie's play *Quality Street* was given over the weekend by the girls of St Martin's High School, Tulse Hill. It was impossible to pick out any one of the girls for special mention as they all pulled together magnificently. It was this co-operation that did so much towards making the School play such a success.'

The Brixton Free Press praised individual major roles and described the play as 'charmingly performed' and 'an undoubted success'. The report ended:

'Reminiscent of the professional English stage was the general excellence of the smaller parts, and the producers, Miss I.D. Free and Miss A.D. Gough, are to be congratulated.'

116

Cast of Quality Street (School magazine 1946)

After the excitement of the play, school settled down to revising for end-of-term exams, working towards a dancing display, and the usual plethora of school activities.

Hockey was now played with enthusiasm from the upper thirds upwards, which meant for many it was a new game. Matches were played against Sydenham High, James Allen, La Retraite and City of London Girls' schools. But after six years of imposed neglect the field was in a poor state. Even so, it was not just the field that was to blame according to a magazine report:

> 'The 1st and 2nd suffered from lack of practice. . .Regular, thoughtful stick-work practice is what all players need.'

In netball, too, played by the lower fourth upwards, players were 'as yet inaccurate'. But soon improvements were made as players worked to pass their "B" test. Matches were played against Grey Coat, Streatham County Secondary, Clapham Secondary and La Retraite schools.

A system of 'Posture Stripes' was initiated in the spring term for 'posture and general neatness and appearance'. To gain this accolade, girls had to walk along a narrow bar while Miss Buzzard, the new gym mistress, called in her quiet, clipped voice, 'Head up, shoulders back, tummy in, tail down.' Over the span of time, the bar was progressively raised after each successful attempt, until perfect posture was achieved and the small, gilt-edged red 'stripe' could be worn with pride.

A diversion from the usually well-organised gym class was related by lower sixth-former Jean Grosse. The tall French windows in the gym were wide open to let in the fresh air, when:

> '. . . there was a sudden shriek, "the cat's got a bird!" It was as good as a hunting cry, and like a pack of hounds in full cry, the whole class gave chase to the offending cat. Terrified, it ran to earth in a stack of charred timbers — once part of our labs. A minute later the cat reappeared without her prey. While a gang of "heavy rescue" set to work to dig out the bird, I dashed after the cat to wreak my vengeance on it. To my amazement I found it just about to spring on a blackbird chick which was lying on the ground.'

Having taken the baby blackbird home, tucked inside her blazer, Jean successfully reared it despite its 'gammy leg', and it returned the following year with its own offspring wanting to be fed!

National dancing became part of the school curriculum in 1946, under Miss Wingrave, a Fellow and Examiner of the Imperial Society of Teachers of Dancing and of the Greek Dancing Association. The spring term culminated in a multi-cultural dancing display, and a spectator enthused:

> 'Despite coupon difficulties the clothing problem was overcome magnificently; old curtains were transformed into skirts, shorts and pieces of braid became very effective Tyrolean trousers, and scarves made delightful headdresses for the Russian peasants. From the back of the hall one could see a kaleidoscope of colour.'

The first summer term of the united school was a busy one. Having seen the advantages of regular swimming lessons at Leatherhead, trips to East Dulwich baths were arranged for some of the senior classes. The following year the whole school would benefit from regular weekly trips to the baths. 'Thus fulfilling an oft-repeated request from the School Council,' said a report.

At the same time, the joy of swimming prompted an ambitious project to save enough money to build the school's own swimming pool. For many years the hallowed words 'it's for the *swimming bath fund*' would be heard, as forms, individuals, parents, Old Girls and friends accomplished all kinds of money-raising efforts towards this aim.

Tennis from form one upwards now took over from netball and hockey, and part of the field was converted to grass courts for extra practice — 'useful for training footwork if not accuracy because of the bumps!' The sixths and lower fifths spent a lazy afternoon at the first post-war Wimbledon championships, and as a report concluded 'this was a great help in enabling them to realize what the game should look like.'

Athletics was added to the PE syllabus under the careful guidance of Miss Buzzard and Miss Imlach when:

> 'All the gymnastics lessons were taken out of doors in the summer to give opportunity for girls to develop suppleness of body and "posture training".'

The whole field came alive with groups of girls occupied at different activities. As part of the 'stamina training', some were skipping, others jog-trotting round the edge of the field. Still more were engaged in sprinting, hurdling, high jumps, long jumps, relay races and even 'javelin' throwing, using long canes.

Although there was a choice in the order in which each activity was undertaken, the scheme was meticulously organised. Beforehand, each girl carefully ruled a post card into columns for the events, then grades achieved could be marked in. This set athletics on a firm footing, as with great enthusiasm girls endeavoured to progress through the grades, gradually completing their cards.

Because of this increase in athletic events, separate sports days were held, one for juniors from transition to upper third and one for the seniors. Eliminating heats beforehand meant only athletics finals and heats for the 'lighter-hearted races' took place on sports days, and Phyllis Holmes recalled:

'Unfortunately we did not have a sports uniform and wore blouses and brown school knickers. This was a constant source of embarrassment on sports day when the school was open to all!'

Despite repeated applications to the School Council for brown shorts to be worn for gym and PE, it was several years before these became part of the uniform.

The drama competition, which had been a haphazard event during war years, was now reinstated in two sections due to the large number of scenes to be acted. This first post-war competition was judged by Miss Woodcock of the Toynbee Hall School of Drama, who gave 'helpful criticism and excellent advice'.

The first meeting of the Parent-Teacher Association took place in the autumn term. This was at the suggestion of Miss Gordon Ewen, after the response to parents' Open Days during the previous term. Over three hundred parents attended the first 'At Home' when they heard a talk by the school doctor.

Another innovation which began in the autumn term was called the '7-day week'. In practice it was a 7-day timetable whereby the first day of term became Day I, and the timetable followed on consecutively in seven-day cycles, discounting weekends. The advantage of this system was to enable more subjects to be taken, though less often than weekly. Yet basic subjects could have more timetable slots allotted where necessary. Although not part of the reasoning, this arrangement gave a more varied week, and instead of saying, 'It's Tuesday, it must be maths. . .' it made girls think about each day. It also enabled each year's parallel classes to move more easily within the three bands for basic subjects.

In November, Prize Day was held at Streatham Baths, so the whole school and visitors could be assembled. Miss Bannister returned to present the prizes, and in reflecting the austere post-war times, her speech had the theme 'make do and mend'. She also emphasised the opportunities that were now available for women, but stressed that much hard work and concentration were needed. 'I do not recommend you to try to do your homework while the wireless is on!' Miss Bannister added.

Votes of thanks and cheering followed the speeches. But the loudest cheers came when a day's holiday was announced. Prize Day became an annual outing — and the anticipated day's holiday was always received with cheers of 'surprise'.

Much to everyone's delight, after the junior school had performed *Snow White and the Seven Dwarfs* to the whole school, they were asked to record part of it at the BBC, to be broadcast later to Denmark. Six girls and Miss Miles were taken by car to Bush House one snowy December morning. Julia Munnings in form one proudly wrote a report for the school magazine in which she said:

> 'When we arrived we saw a very big building, we passed through a maze of corridors twisting and turning with lots of people walking about. At last we came to a room marked "silence" and we were very frightened!'

But their initial nerves did not prevent the girls from enjoying the experience, which ended with lemonade and cakes in the BBC canteen.

Another broadcasting success came when the school was invited to submit a script for one of a series of broadcasts, organised by the BBC through the Council for Education and World Citizenship (CEWC). Sixth-former Doreen Brown was invited to audition with four competitors from other schools. 'It was with great delight that we heard Doreen had been chosen to take part in a future broadcast to young people of our own age in America,' wrote Jeanne Archard, who had accompanied Doreen to the studios.

The full term finished with the prefects' party, which promised to be an annual event. Fancy dress costumes were hurriedly fashioned from blackout curtains, remnants and ancient fancy dresses of pre-war days. Pamela Borders and Jean Inglis, from the upper fifth, described the much-anticipated event:

> 'The day of the party dawned crisp and cold, and by the afternoon a thick layer of snow covered the ground, giving the party a festive air. After the 3.45pm bell everybody donned her chosen attire. The mysterious bundles which had lain all day under desks and in cupboards took shape as pirates, crackers, clowns, cowboys and endless other creatures.'

Then followed 'a delicious tea' in the gym and games throughout the building.

'On returning to the hall we were told that a surprise was in store for us. The first thing we heard was the noise of a drum, and Miss Copland crossed the threshold playing vigorously. "It's the Staff!" was the unanimous shout, and sure enough behind Miss Copland the staff entered, but in the guise of small children. And what an unruly herd they were!'

The severe winter conditions, that started towards the end of January 1947 and continued throughout February, had not been envisaged. Snow fell on snow, impacting on the frozen road surfaces so that driving, and even walking, became hazardous. The newly-nationalised coal industry ground to a halt because coal could not be moved from the pit heads. Heating and lighting were restricted by gas and electricity cuts. A National Emergency was declared.

Travelling to school became increasingly hard and many girls stayed away. But one small band of St Martin's girls, who travelled from Leatherhead on the 7.52 each morning, managed to make the journey. Jenny Russell recaptured one memorable occasion:

'A journey of forty minutes took us three hours, and when we finally got to school all the train girls were taken to the domestic science room and given hot chocolate and fruit cake, [even though] food rationing was still in force. We were allowed to leave school an hour earlier to catch the train home, but I don't think we did much work that day.'

After a final onslaught of snow came floods in March, and St Martin's charity fund contributed £20 to the Lord Mayor of London's Flood Relief Fund. But gradually, as the floods and excitement subsided, life returned to normal.

During the school year visits had been arranged once more. The first had been by a group of lower fifth and some sixth-formers to the Britain Can Make It Exhibition, at the Victoria and Albert Museum. The girls were intrigued by the display of plastic goods and 'new pattern designs for materials'. And they quickly found the almost futuristic model kitchens, arranged with 'new labour-saving devices which included the electric washing-up machine and clothes washing machine.'

The lower fifth also enjoyed a performance of *Macbeth* at the Camberwell Theatre, and Peggy Birch recalled her feelings:

'My friends were just as excited as I was and we could talk of nothing else. At 10.45 we trooped down to the cloakroom for there had been strict instructions that we were to look smart and so there was quite a queue for the mirrors.'

Their diligence was rewarded for when they reached the theatre they realised, with pride, that they and girls from Mary Datchelor's were the only schools to be in uniform.

Earlier in the year, before the snow had fallen, the lower fifth had again donned hats, coats and gloves and queued for a glimpse in the mirror. This time they had set out with Miss Copland and Miss Imlach for Westminster Central Hall, to hear a concert by boys and girls of 'a famous Czechoslovakian Youth Club for the pupils of London Secondary Schools'.

On a wet Thursday in April, 'five lucky people', chosen from the lower fifth, assembled in the front entrance hall for a visit to Westminster. Beryl Ashe and Gwen Richardson recorded the event:

'When we arrived at the Houses of Parliament we were glad to hurry out of the rain into the magnificent hall decorated with mural paintings depicting famous historical events. We were in time to see the Speaker's Procession led by the Sergeant at Arms. The Speaker, wearing his black gown and wig, was immediately preceded by an usher bearing the mace made of wrought burnished brass. While we were waiting to go into the debate . . . a police-man brought us each a slip of paper on which we signed our names, stating that we would not cause a disturbance in the House.'

Because of bomb damage to the House of Commons, parliament sat in the House of Lords, and from the Strangers' Gallery the girls heard part of a debate on the fuel crisis. They enjoyed their afternoon steeped in history; seeing how parliament worked and being caught up in ancient customs and formalities.

The following month an upper fourth group was taken to the National Gallery, where their tour covered the mediaeval and renaissance periods. The group's visit added considerably to their understanding and appreciation of art, and thereafter the National Gallery became an annual visit for upper fourths.

By 1947, substantial parts of the education act of 1944 finally came into being. Education was to be organised into primary, secondary and further educational categories, with the school leaving age raised to fifteen. Local authorities were now required to provide secondary schools which were to be:

'Sufficient in number and equipment to afford for all pupils opportunities for education offering such variety of instruction and training as may be desirable in view of their different ages, abilities and aptitudes.'

Different types of secondary schools would be needed to meet the needs of differing children. The tripartite system of grammar, technical and secondary modern schools emerged, and the LCC's *London School Plan* laid the foundations for future comprehensive organisation.

Under the 1947 reorganisation, St Martin's retained its direct grant status, whereby it kept much of its independence, but there were to be no more half-days on Wednesdays, normally used for sports practice or for girls who had been given a detention. And junior girls could no longer pass straight into the seniors, for the 11-plus examination had arrived.

Lined up on the top court (Panora)

Reorganisation also meant that 'all-age' schools would gradually disappear, as the official requirement stated that primary and secondary ages should be housed in separate buildings. Over the next five years the lowest form in the Preparatory Department disbanded as the class moved up. But St Martin's absorbed the changes as the machinery of education moved on.

The sudden death of the vicar of St Martin-in-the-Fields, the Reverend Eric Loveday, was a great loss to church and school alike. The Reverend Charles Edwards succeeded him and also became chairman of the school governors, thus reviving the pre-war custom of the dual role. At the same time Miss Bannister joined the governing body.

A much prized gift to the school was a new projector, donated by the Parents' Committee. The original, silent projector had been destroyed when the school was bombed. But now the new sound projector was put to good use, as films were hired not just for the Film Society but other meetings too.

The varied interests of the societies were matched by a variety of external visits. A RADA performance of *Twelfth Night* at the Camberwell Palace Theatre started off the autumn term for a group of lower fifths. This was followed by a Swedish display of physical training at the Albert Hall, when fifty St Martin's girls met one October Saturday to watch 'an exhibition of skipping, exercises, balance and apparatus work'. A month later, also on a Saturday, a group of upper fifths and sixth-formers attended a concert conducted by Sir Malcolm Sargent.

When a party from the science sixth visited the Electron Jubilee Exhibition at the Science Museum, to commemorate fifty years of the electron's discovery, sixth-former Margaret Fossey wrote enthusiastically:

'Television, x-rays, radar, wireless valves, the electron microscope — practically all the modern marvels of science, so it seemed, were fundamentally dependent on the electron.'

Another visit, this time to an exhibition of art from India and Pakistan at the Royal Academy, followed in February. Miss Piele gave a talk beforehand explaining many of the exhibits, so the group would have a better understanding of the exhibition. Even so, Celia Coombe in the lower fifth wrote in her report:

'There were things that we could not understand, figures carved in stone, busts, animals, statues, all their secrets hidden with them they were so old. . . When we came to the paintings I immediately voted them the best of the exhibits. The wonderful detail of all the leaves on every tree, the charming figures and exquisite colours were all occasions for amazement.'

An unusual competition, that was judged in March 1948, had been started the previous November, when London schools were entered for a bulb-growing competition run by the Central Bulb Committee of Holland. The prize for one hundred lucky winners was to be a visit to the bulb fields. Members of the upper third and lower fourth at St Martin's bought bulbs and instructions for one penny, then carefully tended each potential exhibit through the cold winter months.

In March a profusion of flowering bulbs — from the puny to the perfect — adorned the hall for initial judging by Miss Gordon Ewen, with a committee of governors and staff. The ten best were entered by the school in a display at County Hall. From the thousands of magnificent blooms, two St Martin's girls won a trip to Holland and two were commended. St Martin's was one of twelve schools that also received a silver medallion.

Maureen Gayther and Hazel Skinner described the bulb fields as 'many-coloured carpets'. Their stay included a visit to a Dutch school, travelling along the canals to see the old buildings, and a reception by the Mayor:

'We did not understand the speeches, but we loved the lights. They were gold with an immense number of candles,' wrote the girls. 'Another day we went through the lovely dyke country to the windmill country which we liked very much indeed.'

One of the greatest post-war concerns was how to build a strong, peaceful future. Current Affairs and Citizenship classes covered many ways in which good citizenship would help to maintain world peace, and sixth-former Sheila Rooke, as magazine editor, included stirring words in her editorial:

'We have a wonderful chance of building a new world, but we cannot do it with dreams and theory alone. We must be willing to take the trouble to do the small, uninteresting things — which though they have no glory surrounding them now, will help to put our dreams into action.'

One form of action had been initiated by Miss Pearce and older girls, who had helped form the Lambeth UNA Youth Section. Members were mostly from St Martin's and the Strand School, but gradually other schools were represented. In praising their work, Miss Gordon Ewen commented, 'There are few better ways of serving the community than this.'

Another way of 'promoting good feeling, without which future peace must remain insecure', Miss Gordon Ewen suggested, was to invite twelve German girls and their teacher to stay with girls from St Martin's. A school in Lübeck had already been 'adopted' by St Martin's after the war, when much-needed clothing and books were collected from time to time by each form and sent to Germany.

At Prayers, Miss Gordon Ewen explained what the proposed visit would mean and that it was more than offering a holiday to girls from another country. St Martin's could play its part, small as it was, in 'shaping the future of the world'. The whole venture took on a new significance and hospitality was eagerly offered. Ages were matched, where possible, with those of the visitors and it was important that hostess families had some knowledge of German, although it was later found that most of the German girls spoke good English.

In Germany money had to be raised for fares and travel permits obtained, before the twelve girls arrived with the only female member of staff, Frau Geldmacher, the art teacher.

Mornings were spent in school following the normal curriculum, but after lunch a coach arrived to take 'the German party', which included the English hostesses, staff and some parents, on visits of historical interest. Parties, early picnics, ballet and theatre trips were also arranged, besides outings organised by the hostesses. Jeanne Archard, the Head Girl, summed up her feelings when she said:

'The three weeks became rapidly passing days of discovery for us all. Perhaps for the first time I became really proud of this country and learned to appreciate the many things I have always taken for granted. Together we learned to understand each other's country and to appreciate each other's point of view.'

After the German girls' visit, the school settled back into its usual routine. It had been a highlight that had touched the whole school and culminated in a concert of piano pieces, unaccompanied folk songs and dance given by the visitors.

The link with Lübeck remained, with exchange visits between the schools in subsequent years. During term time German girls joined in the routine activities of St Martin's and St Martin's girls came to understand the pattern of German education.

For ten years, one of the most colourful characters at St Martin's had been Miss Dadd, the art mistress, whose flamboyant hats for Founders' Day, and striking clothes at all times, caused much excited chatter amongst the girls. Miss Dadd appeared as a breath of fresh air with her relaxed approach and great sense of fun.

Sometimes periods of prep were overseen by her in the biology lab, where the teacher's desk had a large overhead mirror. One afternoon girls in the lower fourth, whose minds wandered off their homework, noticed in the mirror a book of nudes that Miss Dadd was studying. Nudges and giggles went round the class, then repeatedly girls went up to the desk to ask trivial questions, hoping to glimpse the book, but it was hastily covered up as each intruder approached.

Sylvia Collins (née Moakes) remembered rumours abounding that Miss Dadd was 'caught teaching Life Class' using one of the pupils as a model. 'Stark naked,' she added. 'Perfectly normal if you are in the art world, but not quite right at St M's!' Sadly, in December 1948 Miss Dadd died just before her retirement, and the school was deprived of an excellent teacher and a lively personality.

As 1949 loomed near, plans had unravelled for celebrating the 250th anniversary of the school. Lessons, exams, sports matches, society meetings, rehearsals for the school play, visits and talks all continued. But there was a growing feeling of excitement that filtered through — 1949 was going to be different.

6. Widening Horizons: 1949 - 65

During the autumn of 1948, any spare time had been taken up with preliminary readings and rehearsals, culminating in February with six performances of *A Midsummer Night's Dream*. For the double cast and all who worked on or watched the production, it proved a memorable occasion, and raised £100 for the Swimming Bath Fund. Jeanette Ridgeway (née Johnson) recalled the happiness when she wrote:

> 'What a production that was. From the little souls who were fairies dancing on at the beginning to Miss Copland's rousing piano accompaniment, to the thunderous applause from the very proud parents in the audience. . .Miss Sutton (Chemistry), Miss Jesson (Physics), Miss Pearce (History) and Miss Dadd* (Art) all did sterling work with hair, make-up and costumes. . .So many people were involved and it was a resounding success with very good critiques in the local press. . . nothing has ever surpassed the excitement of performing *The Dream* at St Martin's.' [**Sadly, having prepared the scenery, Miss Dadd died before the performances were staged.*]

The excitement of the play had barely died down when the school was caught up in the greater involvement of the Jubilee, to mark the school's 250th anniversary. Members of the Historical Society held readings and rehearsals to select performers for a pageant, written by Miss Gordon Ewen, showing the changing stages of the school from 1699-1933. And everyone became involved in preparing for the School Fair.

The celebrations in July started with an evening for parents, with refreshments 'served on the lawn', then came talks and a short musical programme which included the parents' choir. The following morning the whole school climbed into double-decker buses and travelled up to St Martin-in-the-Fields Church for the Jubilee Service, conducted by the Reverend Charles Edwards, with an address by the Right Reverend Austin Pardue, Bishop of Pittsburgh, USA.

In the afternoon, a ceremony was held to unveil a plaque to commemorate the occasion. Once again, parents, staff, governors, Old Girls and distinguished guests crowded into the hall, with the upper school and representatives from the lower school. Many messages of congratulations and good wishes had been received, including those from the Queen (the present Queen Mother) and Queen Mary.

The short ceremony was followed by the first showing of the pageant, and ended with a display of school work. Each

The old and the new 1699-1949
(School magazine)

form had worked diligently in the previous weeks preparing, arranging and displaying their contributions. The busy day ended with an Old Girls' meeting, when the pageant had its second showing. Old Girls from many eras were able to meet, some having not returned to the school since leaving. A report of the evening said:

> 'Records of OGA meetings only go back to 1915, a mere 29 years in our long history, but as a result of notices in *The Times* and *Daily Telegraph*, letters were received from many Old Girls who were at school in Miss Pullée's time.'

But as far as present girls were concerned, the main event of the Jubilee was the Fair on Saturday afternoon.

Preparations had gained momentum in the weeks beforehand when everyone involved with the school had worked towards this one aim. Between morning showers the final preparations were completed. The sun shone as visitors poured in to see the Fair being opened by an Old Girl from Charing Cross days, the well-known

BBC producer, Audrey Cameron. A magazine report captured the feelings:

> 'And then the Fair was in full swing. There were stalls of all kinds from flowers to horoscopes; there were sideshows and pedlars and guessing competitions and dancing displays. The hunger of the younger visitors could be appeased at the Tuck Shop, while for the grown-ups there was a continuous service of homemade teas in the Gym, where over 1,700 teas were served. Some of the older girls had organised a creche where babies and toddlers were looked after and amused while their mothers could wander unencumbered round the stalls. There was a Baby Show, too, which attracted over seventy bonny babies! A miniature railway, kindly procured by one of the parents, gave very great pleasure to young and old alike.'

In reporting the events the *South London Press* said:

> 'Most exciting of all — a treasure trove, the find being a real pair of nylons.'

Nylon stockings were almost unobtainable in this country, so the hidden treasure proved a popular attraction.

Scenes from *Alice in Wonderland*, scientific experiments, a haunted house, the last performance of the pageant and a final auction of unsold goods completed the biggest public event the school had ever staged. Somehow, after all the excitement, school continued for another ten days of that eventful term, but with the satisfaction of knowing that a further £607.1s.9d had been added to the Swimming Bath Fund from the Jubilee Celebrations.

Because of its long history and association with St Martin-in-the-Fields Church, the school attracted many visitors, and Miss Gordon Ewen remarked:

> 'The numerous visitors from abroad who come to see the School keep us constantly aware of the people, both learning and teaching, in other countries and of the interest that they take in the English educational system.'

But this interest was two-way, because exchange visits were arranged for both staff and girls.

The previous year, Miss Calhoun had joined the school on a short exchange visit from Canada. And in September 1949 Miss Imlach exchanged schools for a year with Miss Newburger from the Van Steuben High School, Chicago. Volleyball, baseball and American folk dancing were temporarily added to the curriculum, together with talks and films on the American way of life. The year ended with a programme of American folk dances and tunes, and readings of Walt Whitman's poetry. But unfortunately for the school, Miss Imlach's visit was to lead to her returning to America to join the Foreign Office in Chicago the following year.

Australian links were forged when Miss Jones exchanged places with Dr Anna Matz from Hobart, Tasmania. Dr Matz remarked that there was 'a pleasant working spirit — good fellowship among the staff and a helpful, friendly attitude from the girls'. She added that they were not all angels up on Tulse Hill, but were kind and gave 'a stranger in their midst' a warm welcome.

Christine McCallan (née Ireson) remembered the time when she was 'no angel':

> 'I particularly remember climbing over the wall into the "boys' approval home" next door to retrieve my netball, and being caught by the headmaster, who took me into his study and phoned Miss Gordon Ewen, who swept in and asked me to explain what I was doing in the boys' home. She and the headmaster pointed out the dangers of a girl entering the premises. My answer was , "Well if it is so dangerous why are they here next to a girls' school?" Much to my surprise, Miss Gordon Ewen smiled and sent me back to St Martin's with no further punishment.'

The General Certificate of Education (GCE), at ordinary and higher level, was introduced in 1950 to replace School Certificate and Matric. The new system enabled success in individual subjects to be recognised, instead of pupils only gaining a certificate if all the prescribed subjects were passed. This resulted in a far more flexible system, with greater choice of subjects. Theory of music exams had been introduced, too. And a solitary violin candidate, Penny Dodman, passed her third and fourth grades.

Music has always played an important part in the life of the School, from singing competitions to beautiful music played before Prayers. Under Miss Copland's careful guidance the Music Club flourished, professional concerts were arranged with outside musicians, and the school orchestra was reinstated after a lapse of eleven years.

The carol service once more became an annual event at St Martin-in-the-Fields Church, and carols were sung by the choir at local churches and old people's homes. Pre-Christmas snow added an air of excitement, and Pamela Hough (née Ibbott) recorded in her diary several snowball attacks by the boys from the Strand School. The entries ended with the satisfied comment, 'Strand boys caught by Miss Gordon Ewen.'

That December, the one-hundred-strong choir recorded six carols to be broadcast in the BBC's holiday programme, *Hello There*. Mercia Gow (lower fifth) described the much-anticipated event:

'After we had practised hard for three weeks, the great day arrived. Choir and reserves assembled in the Hall at 8.40 am, and were checked and re-checked. Then collecting sandwiches and safely negotiating ice-bound Tulse Hill, the choir squeezed into one tram for the journey to Westminster Embankment. Arriving at the Church they met the choir of Archbishop Tenison's School, who were to record with them. . .The recording was introduced by Lionel Gamlin and the short service taken by the chairman of the governors, the Rev Charles Edwards, vicar of St Martin's.'

More carol singing quickly followed, when carols were sung in Trafalgar Square on Christmas Eve, and this became an annual event.

The school choir joined the choir of St Martin-in-the-Fields Church with the band of the Coldstream Guards, to lead the massed singing by the crowds that packed the Square around the towering Christmas tree. Janet Kemp (née Burrows) was later to join in with pride, and remembered:

'Taking part in the carol singing on Christmas Eve in Trafalgar Square, I sang until I was hoarse. I was no singer, but went to swell the numbers in the choir. The feeling of importance as the police cleared a path through the crowds to St Martin's crypt, enabling us to have refreshments and receive a gift afterwards, was tremendous.'

In 1951, the year of the Festival of Britain, towns, villages and schools all over the country celebrated British achievement. For St Martin's the year started with performances of the Greek tragedy *Iphigania in Tauris*. The choice of play, although ambitious, was a result of Greek becoming the first classical language in the lower school. Later in the year, scenes from the play became part of the LCC Education Exhibition for the Festival.

The Festival created an upsurge of interest and enthusiasm throughout the country, when bomb sites, rationing and the drabness of post-war conditions were temporarily forgotten. The Dome of Discovery and the many 'pavilions' became an exciting new world for the thousands of pupils from schools all over the country, visiting the exhibitions on the South Bank. Excitement and enthusiasm were carried back with them, and many 'mini festivals' were arranged in their own schools.

At St Martin's, although lessons continued as girls worked towards their GCE and end-of-term exams, the summer term included preparations for a series of exhibitions and displays, the most ambitious of all being the gym and dancing displays. The annual drama competition became the Festival of Drama, the singing competition became the Singing Festival and an elaborate Art and Craft Exhibition was also staged.

Clay modelling, cloth printing and puppetry had been introduced in 'hobbies' lessons, so examples were displayed in the gym, together with a wide variety of drawings and paintings. Pieces of needlework were exhibited in the hall, where girls demonstrated embroidery stitches and patterns of the finished articles.

But the main events of the school's festival year were the massed gym and dancing displays. Mr Wilson, the groundsman, had marked out the field with intersecting white lines, and 500 girls wearing short white tunics with red buttons — specially made in needlework lessons under the meticulous guidance of Miss Lamb — filed on to the field. With precision timing, the events had been practised, class by class, in normal gym lessons with Miss Buzzard and Miss Imlach, and the impressive display ended with each class kneeling down to form the letters ST MARTINS.

The massed gym display was followed by the newly formed senior and junior gym teams showing their prowess in vaulting and other individual skills. Then came a 'rare treat' described by Margaret Poynter and Celia Coombe:

'Undoubtedly the greatest sensation was caused by Miss Buzzard who, arrayed in boater, white blouse with leg-o'mutton sleeves, black tie and long black skirt, looked as if she had just stepped from a Victorian photograph.'

Miss Buzzard was followed by a line of girls neatly dressed in navy blue blouses and long thick skirts. They came to attention before executing the clockwork commands of their '1890s instructor':

'Arms, legs and bodies moved in perfect timing and at the finish of each movement came the command "Repose", when long hair was smoothed down and curls hastily pulled back to the styles in which Miss Sutton had adroitly manoeuvred them.'

During this interlude the majority of girls changed into national costumes representing six countries, one for each year of the school. In turn the different 'countries' danced and sang their practised programmes around the field.

Most of the music was composed by Miss Copland, and great care had been taken to produce accurate costumes. The finale, St Martin's Dance, was performed by the whole school. The discipline and thrill of working in unison as part of a group was an experience which 500 girls would not for-

'Victorian' gymnastics display (Watt)

get. Miss Gordon Ewen summed up her feelings when she said:

'It was one of those rare occasions when every girl could publicly take part in a common effort for the good of the whole School.'

Once again the summer term's 'high' left ten more days to settle back to routine lessons. But these were interspersed with outings to Kew Gardens and Hampton Court's historical pageant, visits with the party of German girls, now an annual event, tennis matches and the final productions of the drama and singing festivals.

Squeezed into the last week of term was a talk showing the need for volunteers to help the Brixton WVS during the holidays. Several girls offered their services and fifth-former Kitty Browning explained their duties:

'I joined forces with another helper undergoing a "trainee" course, and between us we managed the tea canteen at Norwood House, a home for aged people. On Tuesdays and Thursdays we "operated the meals", which meant that we had to collect hot dinners, provided by Spurgeon's Home in Stockwell, and deliver them at the homes of old people, who looked forward eagerly to our visits. On days when I was not required for outdoor duties, I assisted in sorting into sizes articles of clothing. . . Some were needed for jumble sales and garden fetes; others were packed on shelves for future use.'

Helping with the elderly in the neighbourhood became yet another out-of-school activity, which added to the wider experience of senior girls.

That summer holiday, other senior girls took part in an exchange visit to Germany. Barbara Parsons (née Hazel Brown) remembered her journey from London to Frankfurt, and finally on to the small town of Weilberg:

'We travelled by boat and train through the night on wooden seats, and found it pretty tiring. I remember looking out of the train window in the early dawn and seeing the Rhine for the first time. . . Highlights of the trip were a visit by boat to Limburg, and spending the night at the International Camp on the top of the Lorelei Rock — that was our first introduction to the 'hole in the ground' and mixed washrooms. We were under the care of a master from Wantage High School, and there was one girl on her own from Woodford High School. There was a local festival 'Kirmes', when all the children and the town band walked in procession, and we joined in.'

For children in the fifties 'going abroad' was becoming less of a rare event, and gradually more holidays were organised.

Nevertheless, Jennifer Byers (née Friend) thought school parties called for school uniform, sensible clothes and certainly no make-up for sixth-formers. But travelling abroad began to open up new horizons, and Jennifer was later to record:

'We travelled back overnight enduring hard seats and long waits, but as I stumbled up the road to bath and bed, I knew the holiday had been a significant milestone in my life.'

The unexpected death of King George VI, early in 1952, affected the whole country. At St Martin's, Miss Gordon Ewen called everyone into the hall to make the announcement. In the days that followed, several girls joined the enormous queues stretching along the Embankment from Vauxhall Bridge to Westminster Hall, slowly moving forward to view the Lying-in-State.

For several years, small groups from the science sixth, accompanied by Miss Jesson, had visited the Royal Society. 'Very few schools are invited to attend the display of experiments arranged for the Conversazione,' Angela Dodman explained. But once again St Martin's was 'privileged to receive an invitation'. The girls saw films and many demonstrations, including a wind tunnel to observe insects' flight, new almost indestructible materials made from 'chips of crystal-like substance', and undreamed-of discoveries made the previous year by eminent scientists.

The excitement of the visit was soon over when, with apprehensive feelings, the school heard there would be a major school inspection in May. In a résumé of the week's visit Pat Kessel wrote:

'Miss Gordon Ewen announced the forthcoming inspection with a calmness not mirrored by her hearers. . .The inspectors descended upon us in a body; an unnatural air of quietness pervaded the corridors and stairs, and crept into the cloakrooms. . .During the week our visitors worked unceasingly teaching, making suggestions, demanding reasons and questioning girls and Staff (for a change!) unmercifully. They carefully inspected exercise books, seeming to look particularly at that awful prose, the one I did in a hurry because I wanted to play tennis. . . .and that funny drawing I forgot to rub out. Lessons became surprisingly more exciting and interesting, and certainly more amusing, although a sudden command to translate a piece of unprepared Latin or French was received without enjoyment at the time.'

A school inspection should have taken place every ten years, but due to the war more years had elapsed.

After a gradual process over five years of eliminating the lowest class, the Junior School finally closed at the end of the summer term,

St Martin's at leisure (Gratwick)

Starting in the autumn term, the Senior School no longer used the 'upper' and 'lower' prefixes for classes, since the first year of the seniors now became form one. The letter on the classroom door distinguished between parallel classes as before.

The thrill of knowing that Everest had been conquered, in 1953, could not outdo the equally exciting event of the coronation of Queen Elizabeth. A group of thirty-eight girls travelled up to the Embankment to watch the procession and join other school groups on the wide area reserved for them. But some girls, not included in the school party, had spent the night on the pavement with hundreds of spectators. For third-former Iris Potter, it was a memorable night:

'Although it was past three o'clock in the morning, lights twinkled brightly everywhere, vehicles paraded the street decorated in red, white and blue. A barrel-organ filled the air with haunting melodies. . .Then through the noise of the night, softly at first, then growing louder and still louder, came the strains of *Land of Hope and Glory.* Suddenly the night was filled with the voices of people of many nationalities singing. The rain had started, but the singing went on. What a wonderful picture it made — the crowds, standing erect, singing and singing for sheer joy, while the rain fell steadily, unnoticed by anyone.'

Two more girls who skipped lessons to watch the Coronation, by camping out in the Mall, became the talk of the school when their photograph appeared on the front page of a national newspaper!

The 'highlights' that seemed to dominate each post-war year temporarily alleviated the privations of rationing and restrictions that continued. War damage repairs took many years to be completed and bomb-sites' empty spaces had become tangles of weeds. Only gradually were items taken off ration as supplies became more plentiful. But school dinners remained 'a necessary evil' in the eyes of Anne Rice-Jones, who commented:

> 'The cooks did their best with what was available on the allocated budget and rationing restrictions. . .spam fritters, watery custard, congealed gravy and "frog-spawn" [sago] were memorable to say the least.'

Sheila Watt (née Atkins) remembered 'always being told off by the dinner servers', and one day in particular:

> 'I passed my plate round the wrong side of the post in the middle of the serving hatch. I remember thinking, "Oh, dear, I'll be told off for that". So I pulled back my plate and passed it round the other side, only to find that the server had aimed her scoop of sloppy mashed potato at my first placing of the plate. I got another telling off as they looked at the scoopful sitting on the hatch!'

School dinners, at that time, were seldom popular and a strong mixture of food smells hung in the air.

In rows down the hall, the tables were headed by a senior dinner monitor, or occasionally a member of staff. As soon as a table was full, the dinner monitor said grace and started to eat, which was the signal for the rest of the table to begin. Quiet conversation was allowed, but if the noise rose above the required level a period of silence was called for by the mistress on duty.

During the years of the junior school, when meals were eaten in the cookery kitchen, it had been stressed that it was not polite to gobble down the food. Girls had to follow the example of the mistress at the head of the table, keeping pace with the majority by slowing down or speeding up where necessary. In the seniors the same rule applied but was less often kept.

Officially, no food was allowed to be left, apart from odd scraps of gristle. Unofficially, having coaxed a reluctant eater into swallowing a few more mouthfuls, monitors were generally lenient. Girls from each table were selected to take the pile of empty plates back and scrape any leftovers into a container for pig food — hiding from the mistress on duty unusually large amounts, otherwise the dinner monitor would be reprimanded for allowing too much waste. No one could leave the table until these duties had been performed and a final grace said, then chairs were stacked against the wall.

For a short while 'language tables' at lunch time were introduced, with only a prescribed language being spoken. But after 'passez moi the salt' and similar blends of Franglais, or its German equivalent, were regularly heard, the idea was dropped.

In 1954 the ebullient Mrs Davies retired. To trembling juniors she had seemed fierce and stern, yet equally she had laughed with her pupils and hugged them too. In an English lesson she would march into the silent classroom saying, 'Open your exercise books. If there's one line left leave it, if there are two lines use them.' Girls would hurriedly open their books and be immediately ready to work.

In maths lessons, the first seven girls to solve a given problem were told to 'stand behind'. With seven girls proudly standing behind her desk, on the raised dais, a new problem was set.

But sometimes Mrs Davies could be sidetracked into telling intriguing stories, about living in one of the first flats to get heated water, piped under the Thames from the new Battersea Power Station; or of how she had bought a piece of carpet that had actually been walked on by the Queen at her coronation — on which Mrs Davies was contemplating painting gold footprints! And her animated stories of the Norse gods were long remembered.

With great enthusiasm, members of the Film Society produced their first silent film in 1954. A camera was borrowed from the London Schools' Film Society, and girls were divided into groups, each covering a different aspect of the finished production, *The Mystery of St Martin's*.

With this experience behind them, the next year the Film Society took on the more ambitious project of filming the school's second massed gym display. Glimpses of the display were shown from rehearsals through to the final event. Indoor shots showed the events that led up to the three performances, which sadly were held on dull and dismal days. Afterwards, films continued to be made by borrowing a cine-camera from staff or members of the society.

With each autumn term came a new intake of girls, starting apprehensively on their new school life. Janet Kemp, remembering her own first days at St Martin's, said:

'The building seemed huge and the staff, gliding round in their university gowns, were overwhelming.'

But every year the regular annual events and 'rites of passage' gave girls confidence, as they progressed up the school in now familiar surroundings.

More girls gained GCE certificates, as single subjects could be taken. The number gaining secretarial certificates increased, too, and requests for St Martin's-trained girls were often received. At the same time, those achieving Higher Certificates and gaining university entrance also increased. Sheila Watt vividly recalled her A levels in 1956, because she had chosen to take French, German and Pure Maths, a combination of arts and science which caused problems, as she explained:

'When I came to the exams, a maths paper clashed with a language one. I therefore sat one paper in the morning, was escorted to the library, which was closed, to have lunch and stayed on my own till it was time to be escorted back to the exam room to do the other morning paper in the afternoon.'

In the summer of 1956, builders, scaffolding and upheaval once more descended on the school. Soon after the war a temporary roof had been erected over laboratories and art room, but now a more permanent one was to be built. Once again, as in wartime, the church hall was used for lessons, while science classes were held in form rooms and the cookery kitchen.

An unusual event in the autumn term was Museum Week, organised by Miss Pearce and Miss Meyer to mark International Museum

Week, sponsored by UNESCO. The corridors displayed pictures and details relating to many of the world's great museums. An information centre was positioned by the gym, while the library had catalogues, leaflets and a display of loaned artifacts and photographs.

Competitions were arranged to encourage interest, and each form had two history lessons in which to study the exhibits. The school stayed open until 4.30 each day so that girls had a further opportunity to find answers to the competitions. Museum Week was a resounding success, not only in helping to raise the profile of national and local museums, but as a fascinating history project for the whole school.

At this time, a new school badge was designed by Miss Austen Reeves, the art mistress. It depicted St Martin handing half his cloak to the beggar, from the ancient legend, with the motto, *caritate et disciplina*. This replaced the original motto, *mind measures man*, which seemed inappropriate for a girls' school, especially as 'man', short for 'mankind' had become outmoded.

Because of a need to increase the school's endowment, an Appeal Fund was launched in 1957, with a target of £100,000. Over subsequent years this would enable a programme of building to be undertaken for new facilities. And once again, parents, Old Girls, governors and the school organised events to raise the essential money.

The first of these was a re-showing of the school pageant. The ending was brought up to date, and over eighty girls and many members of staff worked together to produce five performances, which raised £150 for the Appeal Fund.

The OGA set themselves a target of £1,000 towards the fund after Miss Sutton had posed the question, 'What is it worth to me to have been a member of St Martin's?' The following year a sale of wines and spirits, organised by the school at the Vintners' Company Hall, was a well received project which added over £400 to the fund. And so, once more, the school set about individual and joint activities to raise money over and above the regular charities which annually raised around £100. But the Charities Fund was a longstanding, separate endeavour, involved with many different organisations as diverse as the Pestalozzi Foundation and polio research.

In 1958 Miss Copland, the much-loved music teacher, retired after thirty years at St Martin's. In her appreciation, Miss Gordon Ewen wrote of her:

'Over all these years the school has been the first interest in her life and all her musical talent has been at its disposal. She built up a reputation for our school choir that has reached far outside the building; she has delighted us with the beauty of her playing; she has warmed us with her goodwill.'

The new music teacher was destined to carry on with the same enthusiasm.

Quietly, Miss Hyde involved herself in the Music Society, choir and concerts as the well-laid musical tradition of the school continued. A major innovation to the musical programme came when the choir joined with the choir of St Martin-in-the-Fields Church at Easter to sing Bach's *St John Passion*. 'It was an experience we shall never forget,' said one sixth-former.

The Living in Lambeth Exhibition, organised by the Lambeth Borough Council, brought more fame to St Martin's and many schools in the district, including Dick Sheppard the school's near neighbour. The general and secretarial sixths, under the guidance of Miss Pearce, worked for many weeks preparing their exhibits, which had the theme Lambeth Industry — Yesterday and Today. History lessons were taken up with visits to bronze works, libraries, potteries, glass works and a bakery.

'As the months passed, our material began to build up and we set about transforming it into charts and diagrams suitable for public display,' wrote Penelope Van der Gucht, Victoria Humphries and Pat Shepherd. 'Perhaps the greatest moment of the whole enterprise was when television cameras came down to film our work.'

A surprise announcement, in July 1959, was that St Martin's had been accepted as an official Church of England School. Because of its connections with St Martin-in-the-Fields Church and the SPCK, this had always been assumed. Despite this potential financial support for the buildings, the Appeal Fund continued to be needed and a staggering £1,000 was raised in a raffle for a car.

Another money-raising activity raised over £200, when the parents' committee organised a school fair and raffle, to buy the school's first television set. Initially, this was to be used by the sixth form, mainly for maths projects, but later the whole school had access to it.

The swimming bath fund continued, too, for the target had not quite been reached. However, with the confidence of money raised and more still to come, the governors at last gave authority for the architect to go ahead with the plans. The site was finally marked out at the side of the field, and work started in the summer term of 1960. The following year a piece of adjacent land, owned by Trinity Rise church, was bought for later school development, and gradually the school campus began to change.

First came a large, airy dining hall extending from the lower cloakroom over the original 'top court'. This was quickly followed by the completion of the swimming bath, with its official opening in October 1962. From the original estimate of £5,000, the cost had risen to £25,000, but it was described by a national swimming coach as 'one of the finest school baths in London'.

> 'There was great excitement as girls stepped, slipped and plunged into the beautiful pale blue water, which, thanks to the LCC was marvellously heated, as was the air in the surrounds and dressing rooms,' a report enthused.

Weekly swimming clubs, team practices and after-school times for staff, Old Girls, parents and friends were all slotted in. The dream of over thirteen years had at last been realised.

Even so, still more money was needed and sixth-former Jennifer Bentall described the swimming bath fund as a 'bottomless gorge with an insatiable appetite for money'. To remedy this, as a final, all-out effort to clear loans and pay for inevitable 'extras', a consolidated money-raising fortnight was arranged in the spring term of 1964. Sixth-former Janet Mills recounted that during Swimming Bath Fortnight:

> 'Individuals cleaned shoes and cars, ran errands and jumble sales, weeded gardens, minded babies, made sweets and cakes, gave film shows, and one girl even organised a children's club. One of the sixth forms ran a dance which was both a social and a financial success.'

Three swimming evenings were arranged, too, with demonstrations by all sections of the school, to an audience of parents and friends.

To round off the fortnight came five performances of *Trial By Jury*, the school's first Gilbert and Sullivan production. Despite lack of facilities due to the building work, the enthusiastic staging proved to be a 'magnificent kaleidoscope of colour and music'.

In July another official opening took place, this time for refurbished laboratories, classrooms, domestic science, art, medical and music rooms and the extended, 'gleaming and resplendent' hall. While alterations had been rapidly taking shape, members of the new Art Society had sketched the many changes. These added to the displays of work and exhibitions arranged throughout the school, for visitors who crowded in to see the refurbishments.

Afterwards, the school was not completely free from builders because work continued with the finishing touches — a need that had been 'miraculously camouflaged by potted plants'. Later that year the original old building of Silwood House was to be underpinned. During all the building processes, school had 'valiantly carried on around the builders' as once again St Martin's learnt to adapt. Summing up her years at St Martin's, Bridget Glanville (née Heard) said:

> 'Every day for morning assembly, over 500 girls from eighteen rooms reached their places in the hall without collision. Every year, at the prizegiving, held at Streatham Baths, staff, pupils and parents were accommodated without fuss and, thanks to the time and trouble taken by Miss Buzzard and other staff in rehearsing the prizewinners in the art of crossing the platform, proceedings ran smoothly. Twice a year the whole school was taken to St Martin-in-the-Fields' Church for Carol and Founders' Day Services. Every few years a gym display involving the whole school was held. Whatever may have gone wrong during lessons and rehearsals, everything ran smoothly on the day.'

A fashion show also 'ran smoothly on the day' towards the end of the summer term. Presented in the dining hall, it ably displayed the work of the first and second year girls. This included summer skirts, dresses and fashionable 'baby-doll' pyjamas.

To round off the term came an afternoon of music. Folk songs, solo singers and instrumentalists and rousing choruses by the whole school combined to create a lively end-of-term event, in the newly enlarged and redecorated hall. Music of a different kind was appreciated when Miss Hyde — who became Mrs Wright in the summer holidays — arranged for the Music Club to go to a promenade concert conducted by Sir Adrian Boult.

In the autumn term, twelve girls, including two guitarists, were selected from the choir to record songs and instrumental pieces. The programme, interspersed with information about the pieces, was to be taped and later played to junior schools. The idea had been suggested by Mr Hodgson, head of LCC drama, who had adjudicated the school's drama competition in the summer term. And the day soon came when he set up recording equipment in the school hall.

'With knees quaking, we stared up at the microphone as if to some domineering monster, waiting for the introduction to finish and our cue to come,' wrote Christine Bailey. 'We eventually began, carefully counting the bars to our entry, and we made it! Every song went well, even the solos, and the instrumental pieces had never sounded more polished. The hall, being closely guarded, was never intruded upon, and the school, marshalled by the staff, kept the silence.'

A visit from a London barrister, that autumn term, set in motion a scheme by the fifth and sixth years for visiting local old people. Members of staff made initial visits to see who would like a regular visitor to chat or for odd jobs.

'One member of staff had something thrown at her from a window,' reported Christine Bailey, 'and was about to turn away, thinking she was not wanted, when she realized it was a door key!'

Many jobs were undertaken, including ironing, shopping and letter writing, while the rest of the school raised money for decorating materials, and contributed groceries and blankets.

Hearing of the scheme, the Roufell Park Good Samaritans undertook the decorating projects, and help was also provided by the Lambeth Welfare Services. But it was the regular visits, made in the lunch time or after school, that were most welcome, and from the initial fifteen local residents, the number visited rose to over fifty.

Christine Bailey finished her report by expressing:

'We owe our thanks to the old people themselves, for from them we have gained at least as much as we have given.'

And so to 1965, when Miss Gordon Ewen's retirement was announced. Miss Gordon Ewen's firm, but sympathetic understanding, and her almost regal appearance in the eyes of new girls, had created the awe in which she was held. But as girls moved up the school they learnt to respect her for her fairness as well as her firmness. After twenty-three years as headmistress, and having been connected with St Martin's since Charing Cross days, the school decided to present a special farewell afternoon for her at the end of the summer term.

In the meantime, Miss Buzzard's retirement was also announced. Miss Buzzard had been a pioneer of athletics for girls throughout the country, and had considerably raised the standard of physical training in the school. She had also been a tireless force behind the long years of money-raising for the swimming bath. So another afternoon entertainment was planned, this time to coincide with Miss Buzzard's birthday in July. School activities progressed with an undercurrent of excitement, as the two 'afternoons' were secretly planned. With school exams over, organisation began in earnest.

The first part of Miss Buzzard's entertainment was in the school hall, where everyone was assembled to watch a series of humorous sketches depicting the history and rules of hockey. Afterwards, Miss Buzzard was presented with a book containing the commentary and pictures from the sketches. The book was entitled This is Your Game. Everyone then walked down to the swimming pool for a variety of swimming and diving displays. The afternoon ended with the whole school singing *Happy Birthday*.

A week later, Miss Gordon Ewen's 'afternoon' started with scenes depicting the school's long history, written and produced by the sixth form, with a cast of over a hundred representing each year of the school. As the last scene ended:

'. . .attention was drawn to the back of the hall, as slowly towards the stage came a trolley bearing a three-tiered cake, magnificently decorated, again the work of the school, in this case the sixth form,' wrote Honor Smith. 'When the cake reached its destination, there was a splendid moment when out of the bottom tier popped a first-former, who presented Miss Gordon Ewen with a ceremonial knife.'

Individual form presentations followed, including a dressed doll in full St Martin's uniform, and a tape recording of sounds of the school covering every aspect of school life, 'even the sound of the staff room at break!'

The fifth form had compiled a book of sketches of the school and an original essay or poem from 'every member of every form'. The afternoon ended when Miss Gordon Ewen was conducted down to the field and 'settled fairly securely on the top of an umpire's chair'. Then on to the field ran the girls to form the letters MISS G E ST MARTINS THANKS YOU. It was an afternoon which 'none of us who took part will ever forget,' concluded Honor Smith.

Mr and Mrs Jones, the caretakers who had looked after the school since it arrived at Tulse Hill, made the break in July, too. Mrs Jones' sister, the indomitable Blake, having helped in so many ways at Tulse Hill, had retired two years earlier.

Miss Gordon Ewen's successor, Miss Joan Mangold, wrote:

'Seldom can an incoming headmistress have had the way prepared for her with so much kindness, so much competence and so much imagination. Miss Bannister, too, invited me to her home; the staff did everything possible to help, as did the Parents' Committee, and I was quickly made to feel "one of the family".'

With the new head, more changes were to come as the life of the school and its traditions flowed on.

7. Adapting to Change: 1965 - 89

The year 1965 had been a busy one. It ended, that crowded autumn term, with sixth-form geography field trips to Yorkshire, Devon and Shropshire. There had been a French verse speaking competition; a visit to Oakfield School, West Dulwich, to see *Theatre Go Round* showing the history of drama; a Parents' Fair at school and stalls at the St Martin-in-the-Fields Church Fair and the Refugee Fair. The senior school won the Lambeth Road Safety competition for the third year in succession and there were rehearsals and productions of *A Winter's Tale*.

Finally, profits from the sixth-form dance, 'generally accepted to be one of the best school dances', paid for a Christmas tree for the school and later bought new science equipment, as well as providing an old people's party in the spring. This then became an annual event.

Membership of the Council for Education in World Citizenship (CEWC) enabled senior girls to attend the New Year four-day conference at Central Hall, Westminster, when young people from all over Britain and many parts of the world met to discuss world problems. Honor Smith described the atmosphere as 'rather like that of the Proms, exceedingly friendly and crowded'. The theme for 1966 was Race Against Time, when 'some really serious and useful work was done'.

Other lectures were those arranged by the LCC, (now the Inner London Education Authority [ILEA]), which seniors had attended for several years during the Christmas holidays,

A 'rite of passage', marking the stepping stones of life, was the Duke of Edinburgh's Award. Since its inception in 1956, senior girls worked at varied activities for their Bronze, Silver and Gold awards. Successful completion meant a visit to Buckingham Palace to be presented with a Gold Award certificate by Prince Philip. The scheme provided:

'An introduction to worthwhile leisure activities and voluntary service, as a challenge to the individual to discover the satisfaction of achievement.'

And each different group of girls continued to 'learn by experience the importance of commitment, enterprise and effort'. Sixth-former Margaret Harris described the award ceremony as one of the highlights of her life.

Opportunities for girls had greatly increased over the post-war years. In 1966 fourteen girls went on to university, which had now become an accepted aim. Six more sixth-formers went to colleges of education (the new name for teacher training colleges), and six to colleges of art, music or law. Thirty-nine girls achieved A levels compared with seven when GCE was introduced fifteen years earlier. The secretarial sixth had maintained good results as well, with the number of certificates being nearly doubled for shorthand and typing, while office practice and commerce had also been introduced.

Girls were learning the violin, viola, 'cello, double bass, flute, clarinet and oboe. Later the bassoon was added. Music certificates had almost trebled compared with 1951, and many girls played in the school's senior or junior orchestras. Some extended their interest by belonging to local orchestras, too. Catherine Sydee, Janet Austen and Old Girl Hilary Wiltshire were members of the London Schools' Symphony first orchestra. Linda Tyrrell, in the second orchestra, was also a member of a group of young people who played in the Lambeth Schools' Music Association's annual concert.

With music a major interest, at the end of the summer term the school enjoyed an afternoon of folk songs, solos, percussion, guitar and piano pieces. The rousing finale was a piece played by the combined choirs and school orchestras.

Although the range of job options was becoming broader, nursing, teaching and secretarial work still dominated the chosen careers. A few leavers found jobs in speech therapy, surveying, marine engineering and the Police Force, while Christabel Sharp was the sixth woman in Britain to gain the Board of Trade Yachtmaster's certificate. Working in a bank became a popular choice, possibly because, as one bank stated, 'In most jobs you have to be *better* than a man to enjoy his opportunities (and his pay).' But not, apparently, in banks where the annual salary started at £360 for a sixteen-year-old, and rose to £445 at eighteen.

During the autumn term of 1966, St Martin's entered a team in the BBC's Top of the Form general knowledge quiz. After close eliminating rounds with City of Bath Boys', Crewe Girls', the Academy of Boys, Edinburgh, and finally Cardiff Boys', St Martin's team was delighted to be awarded the new edition of *Encyclopaedia Britannica* and a Top of the Form cup. The team successfully competed against an Old Girls' team the following year.

Losing to James Allen's, in a competition organised by the English Speaking Union, did not deter the popularity of contests and competitions. And interest in debating increased when a St Martin's team of three came third out of seventeen, in a schools' debating competition held at Lambeth Town Hall.

A lively debate, with Tulse Hill School, discussed the controversial topic 'The woman has become the predominant partner in a relationship'. The following month, a debate held at Emmanuel School proposed 'This house would support the return of an absolute monarchy'. It was the staff's turn to join the debaters in the summer, with the subject 'Guy Fawkes had the right idea'. Unfortunately the outcome of these debates was not reported.

At this time, the school magazine was completely revamped. Gone was the small brown magazine, with its flame coloured stripe along the spine, which had kept the same format for nearly forty years. In its place came a larger, more expansive product, with career-orientated advertisements to help pay for the additional cost. The 1967 editor, Amina Patel, said:

> 'The school voiced its approval of the new style of presentation and suggested methods of improvement. . .This renewed interest in the magazine was not confined to pupils, for several Old Girls offered their opinions and some constructive criticism.'

In many ways, St Martin's horizons were broadening. Whereas visits to Russia had seemed an unattainable dream, now, during the summer holidays of 1967, a party of seven sixth-formers went on a two-week exchange visit. Their first week was packed with sightseeing in Moscow, where the girls' mini skirts — in vogue in Britain — were viewed with interest when the party walked in Red Square.

For the second week, the party attended a mixed Pioneer Camp 'in the depths of a forest'. The camp, described as a rest, had a vigorous programme of exercises on the parade ground before breakfast, games of table tennis, volleyball and basketball, dancing and singing until 2am followed by fishing two hours later. After a return visit was made by the Russian girls to England, Marion Chesney and Dorothy Brennan wrote:

'Following a hectic week of sight-seeing the Russian pupils came into our homes. They all seemed to appreciate this as it gave them an opportunity to relax and let the tempo of life slow down. . .we did try to give a broad view of English life, but it is hoped that in future exchange visits the Russian pupils will become more outspoken and tell us what they really think and feel.'

Marion and Dorothy also noted that 'on their arrival in England, the Russian girls had shortened their skirts considerably'. The much enjoyed Russian exchange visits, organised by Lambeth Borough Council, continued for several years.

After the GCE exams had been established, a Department of Education committee had been set up to look into the possibility of further examinations to broaden the scope for a wider range of abilities. Thus, the Certificate of Secondary Education (CSE) came into being fourteen years after the first GCEs were taken. St Martin's didn't at first follow this course, but in 1968 nine girls received grade one certificates in history, Spanish and French, and thereafter CSEs became an option for extra subjects.

With the general relaxing of attitudes in the 'swinging sixties', it could not be long before St Martin's began to follow the trend of less rigid conformity. Mini skirts in Moscow, demonstrations of cosmetic skills for the fourth, fifth and sixth forms, discos not dances, wider interests and horizons, all reflected a new freedom — with definitely no school uniform out of school. Gowns, too, were 'out', only being worn on speech days and for Prayers by Miss Mangold.

Art was one way in which this freedom could be expressed, and the Youth Summer Art School held at Slindon House, in West Sussex, was voted 'a great success artistically and socially'. At first, fifth-year Claire Knope and Lynn Harris were 'rather disappointed by the lack of facilities and the general chaos'. But apprehensions were soon overcome as they realised the 'spartan conditions' were perfect for 'experimenting without fear with messy paint'. The month's course covered still life, life drawing, landscape and general projects, plus visits in the area.

> 'At the dance on the last night everyone vowed to attend the course again next year,' wrote Claire and Lynn.

Despite the more relaxed attitude of young people, a census carried out in school, on a representative cross-section of girls, agreed by 99% that school uniform should stay. Many girls supported the idea of a basic skirt, blouse and jumper in standard colours of brown, beige and red. But it was pointed out to the girls who organised the census that it was a privilege of sixth-formers to wear a skirt instead of a pinafore dress, which had earlier updated the gym tunic.

> 'The most criticized part of the uniform was the hat,' the report stated, 'which provides a target for ridicule from roving bands of hostile little boys.'

This prompted the comment 'Let's have stronger elastic in the hats!' Instead, St Martin's girls left school at 3.50, before the rush of boys from Tulse Hill could 'ping' the hats or use them as objects to throw or kick, so hats stayed for a few more years.

The standard of swimming and diving had gradually been raised since the school swimming pool had been opened, and inter-form galas were held each year in the summer term. Girls worked for their Schools' Medallist and Advanced Medallist awards, and many achieved bronze, silver or gold personal survival awards. In 1969, seventy-six girls received a merit and five were awarded the advanced medal for speed swimming.

Junior and senior teams were matched in close contests against

Wimbledon High, Clapham County, Mary Datchelor, La Retraite and Dick Sheppard schools. And a 'very loyal bunch of swimmers and divers' spent much time during and after school practising. If two qualified teachers were not available for a swimming lesson, another member of staff had to stand in during her 'free' to watch the pool and make sure no one got into difficulties while the instructor's back was turned.

All was going well until 1970. Then, to everyone's consternation, problems with the structure of the pool began to appear. At first these were thought to be minor, but gradually opportunities to use the pool became uncertain.

As a result, greater interest was shown in athletics, and once again rounders was introduced. Extra attention given to athletics led to more training, and later both the junior and senior teams reaped rewards in the South London Athletics Championships. Grace Bailey went on to create a new London Junior Girls' long jump record of 15ft 9ins. But problems with the pool were to last, and other pursuits began to be given more time as a report indicated:

> 'For the first time in its history, our girls joined the ranks of the many who were already struggling around the muddy cross-country courses of South London. Despite their relative inexperience our team came 4th. They then represented the borough in the "All-London's" where they finished in 2nd place.'

A big change throughout the country came in 1971, when decimal money was introduced. Old pennies and shillings were replaced with decimal coins, although the shilling continued to be used as 5p for some time. Those learning maths through the old system now had to make a radical change in their thinking.

An ambitious venture for the school was skiing, first at Kandersteg during the Christmas holidays, and the following year in the Austrian Tyrol. Skiing sessions in the gym and 'hilarious visits' to the Crystal Palace ski-slope, with resultant aches and pains, had prepared the groups of sixth-formers.

As soon as they arrived, the first group made friends with a party of boys from a Cornish grammar school who were sharing the hotel.

The daily programme was full and varied, with days divided between practice time, two-hour skiing lessons and excursions to local beauty spots or shopping trips. For the intrepid travellers:

'The highlight of the week was New Year's Eve when we were introduced to the Swiss new year customs and similarly we introduced them to "Auld Lang Syne".'

After exhausting coach journeys and the flight home, both parties returned to school the next morning to resume their lessons, but their minds were on the snow, the brilliant sunshine and thrills of skiing.

Outings to Box Hill had become a regular feature each spring term for fieldwork trips. Later, Mrs Jean Orton (geography) wrote:

'The girls regarded it as a fun outing, if somewhat strenuous, but we packed as much chalk scenery, map work and river study as we could into that one day, and then milked it to the last drop back in the class to satisfy the fieldwork requirements for O level. A level students were sent off to residential courses run by the Field Studies Council at their own centres. This was a valuable experience for them, and provided specialist teaching which we could not have hoped to match.'

At the beginning of the summer holidays, in 1972, Mrs Orton organised her own fifth-year residential field course, in the Lower Wye Valley. Its success prompted another residential course the following Easter, when her husband accompanied the group:

'Unfortunately, propriety dictated that he sleep in one of the cabins in the grounds; they were unheated and it snowed!' Mrs Orton remembered.

Despite this propriety, life was changing as the voices of 'women's lib' were increasingly heard.

In the annual public speaking competition held at school, with teams from the fifth and sixth forms, the subject of women's liberation was forcefully aired by proposer and opposer. Other subjects argued ranged from 'The sixth form should take over the school' to 'The merits and disadvantages of chewing gum'. But the women's lib proposer, Ruth Brown, won the contest.

With the rise of interest in public speaking and debating, the sixth forms had attended several debates at Tulse Hill School with the Strand boys and Dick Sheppard girls. Because of this interest, St

Martin's sixth re-started their own debating society, tackling such controversial subjects as 'Women's Inferiority' and 'The maxi skirt will dampen the male spirit'.

Gender questions came up again in a series of magazine articles on 'Women's Lib – For and Against'. The final article putting forward a male view ended:

> '. . .so if the woman rules the man, we may live to see the day when a woman becomes a prime minister, sports commentator, newscaster, principal conductor etc. . .Nonsense!'

Equality of job prospects may not have arrived, but girls and boys were mixing more freely compared with the days when girls were forbidden to speak to boys in the street, and school dances were strictly girls only events.

Mixing together, particularly for sixth-formers, took on greater significance when the school-leaving age was finally raised to sixteen. This was first seen as a probability in the late thirties.

Educational visits became more varied in the seventies, with regular geography, biology and ecology field trips. Day trips to France and further skiing holidays were arranged, and after a month's excursion by transit van to Greece, the girls returned 'clutching duty-free drink and cigarettes'. Pony trekking in Wales was a new venture for a group of fifth years who wrote:

> 'The afternoon brought our introduction to the horses and we went for a two-hour trek. . .For the last few days we covered about 50 miles, and George (an instructor) came with us shouting, "Right rein left leg, and close up them gaps. Put the boot in! Don't let your ponies drink.". . .We cantered, hanging on for dear life, with feet hanging and stirrups flying everywhere. Jane completely lost her stirrups which Kevin (another instructor) rescued from a three foot ditch and then retied them on with string.'

But the report concluded:

> 'On arriving back at St Martin's we realised just how much we wanted to go back to Wales.'

As wider horizons opened up, involvement in school societies waned, until gradually they were overtaken by other activities. The societies had played an important part in school life, and over the years had received an enthusiastic response. For many girls, interests that started through the societies proved to be life-long.

Laying the foundations for a new library had started in the autumn term of 1973, and by the following April the magnificent new building was completed. Miss Mangold described it as 'a building of quiet distinction'. With its attractive arches, carpeted flooring, wooden balustrades and curving staircase leading to the gallery area, it provided an atmosphere of 'dignity and repose'. Fifth-former, Francis Priest commented:

> 'Even those who, like me, have been sitting for ages propped most uncomfortably against a jutting, rickety, overloaded bookcase, must now admit it was worth it to have all those books reclining about the school in the most unorthodox of places. The library is finished! Now it is something new and marvellous, something white and clean and gracious, while we wait anxiously to dive in and use it.'

And soon girls were 'diving in to use it', to select new titles or browse through the growing number of new books.

The old library, above the main entrance in the old part of the building, was quickly converted to a sixth-form common room where girls could relax and chat or revise in peace. Tea and coffee making facilities added to the feeling of independence, and of being just a little apart from the main body of the school. More girls were staying on into the sixth and upper sixth, and these changes reflected their more mature status.

Throughout the school's long history, discipline had been firmly maintained. School uniform was regularly checked and occasionally adapted. In 1974 a new Donny Osmond style corduroy peaked cap replaced the brown beret, and was greeted with both delight and derision. Homework was strictly enforced, with increasing amounts set each night as girls progressed up the school. Homework not handed in or badly done could result in a detention held after school, but parents had to be given at least a day's prior warning so they would know of the late homecoming.

The major event of 1974 was the school's 275th anniversary. After the Founders' Day Service at St Martin-in-the-Fields Church the school returned to Tulse Hill for a summer fair, opened by the Mayor of Lambeth. The first and second years marched on to the field to form the school's name depicted in brown and flame. Then followed sideshows, a concert and plays. In the evening, the home economics department organised barbecue suppers and the busy day ended with a dance.

Two years after the school's celebrations, St Martin's church celebrated the 250th anniversary of the present building. The original far smaller and simpler church, that had raised money from its parish to start a charity school, had been rebuilt in 1726. To mark this anniversary, an exhibition was staged in the crypt from June until November. The school's contribution was a display covering the architectural history of the church, with drawings, paintings and maps created by girls from all forms, under the guidance of the Art Director Miss Austen Reeves.

Creating an interest on Saturdays was part of the reason for the new Rambling Club, formed by the geography staff. Mainly girls from the lower and middle school joined, because many older ones had Saturday morning jobs. By 8.30 on an early autumn morning:

> 'Brightly clad figures assembled around Miss Matthews in the station forecourt, welly-booted and stoutly shod, clutching variously shaped bundles of food. St Martin's Rambling Club was departing for yet another assault on the unsuspecting Surrey Hills.'

After flooded roads, mud, pounding down flinty tracks, the marvels of a 'misty vista', a peaceful picnic and negotiating both fallen trees and a flock of sheep, the party eventually returned to Box Hill Station, only to find the train had gone and the only shop was shut. Even so, they all agreed 'it was a good day out, anyway!' And the Rambling Club enjoyed many similar excursions.

Yet another new venture, this time for third-formers, was a week on the *Sir Allen Herbert* barge, sailing in the Thames estuary. But while girls worked and played, behind the scenes Miss Mangold, staff and governors were involved with the intricacies of organisation, as they started preparing for an even greater change in the life of the school.

Comprehensive education had been introduced in some areas as early as the 1950s. In the sixties and seventies it gained momentum, and by 1976, with the passing of a new education act, St Martin's knew that the following year the structure of the first-year intake would change to include a broad range of abilities, when the 11+ exam would no longer be taken.

A busy period of adjustment was envisaged, while the school prepared for the many changes that would arise, and through endless discussion, plans began to be laid. In the meantime, the school carried on with its familiar routine and occasional highlights, one of which was the first school cruise.

Excitement mounted as December approached and a group of sixth-form girls and three teachers prepared for their travels aboard SS *Uganda*. At six in the morning, the sleepy party gathered at school and boarded a coach for Gatwick airport and the flight to Naples. Elaine Parker described their eventful holiday, which started by losing two cases from the back of the coach:

> 'We drove round Croydon, went to the police but could not find them. We were so late by then that we continued on to Gatwick, to be met by one of the girl's parents who had picked up the stray cases from the middle of the road.'

The holiday had begun!

In Italy they explored the back streets of Naples, before moving on to experience the magnificence of Pompeii. Interspersed with lectures and deck games, the cruise reached Alexandria where the school party was welcomed by an Egyptian brass band. Arab traders bombarded the girls with shouts of 'many bargains — very cheap', before they could move on to see the towering Pyramids and beautiful sunsets. Cyprus, Izmir, Ephesus, Santorini's volcanic crater, the wonders of ancient Greece were eagerly visited, and finally came the flight back from Brindisi – memorable days packed into their crowded holiday.

A later school cruise on *SS Uganda* was not so fortunate. Due to bad weather the ship was unable to dock at Alexandria, so there could be no visit to the pyramids. Further disappointment came when the captain announced that he was having difficulty steering the ship. This time Rhodes and Crete were missed from the itinerary.

School cruise on SS Uganda (School magazine 1981)

Bad weather and long delays dogged the unfortunate cruise; even so the girls enjoyed a varied programme, if not all that had been planned.

Through the years, travel abroad and at home had helped history and geography to come alive. Films, slides and visual aids augmented this first-hand experience. But it was some time before Mrs Orton's geography classroom was fitted with a pull-down projector screen and proper blackout curtains. She remembered:

> '. . .the first overhead projector we acquired, a great heavy thing which had to be trundled round the school to wherever it was needed, and in my case manhandled up the stairs.'

When a second television set had been procured, more forms were able to see educational programmes. An early video recorder made taping programmes possible, but with no preset timer, recording was often at inconvenient moments. Mrs Orton had attended courses for using the equipment, so she was put in charge of visual aids:

'. . .which meant everything from ordering new duplicator paper to being called out of lessons to stand over a man while he fixed a machine. Eventually this area expanded so much we got a Media Resources Officer, who looked after the equipment and would even design and print booklets and worksheets for you, if you told him what you wanted. Such luxury!'

Visits to exhibitions and museums continued, and the Latin group visited the Pompeii exhibition which reinforced memories for those who had been on the school cruise. There were study days at the Victoria and Albert Museum for A level French and English groups, and visits to the Ideal Home Exhibition for O level cookery.

Even more popular, and dominating the spring term of 1977, were rehearsals for *HMS Pinafore* with Alleyn's School. Joint Gilbert and Sullivan performances at Alleyn's the previous year had been so successful that this became an annual event. At first the two schools stayed in separate groups:

'What we didn't know was that the boys gathered in the Buttery at the end to give us marks. Cheek!' commented the indignant St Martin's girls. 'Did they also give the Producer (Deputy Head of Alleyn's) marks for his solo dance when he demonstrated how demure young ladies (that's us) should "gaily trip in"?'

Rehearsals started in January, and after Easter extended to Sunday afternoons. Costumes arrived early in May, when three girls dressed in full Regency attire went off to the sweet shop to stock up, much to the amazement of other shoppers and passing drivers. But once again, successful performances promised future Gilbert and Sullivan productions at Alleyn's.

Between bouts of closure for swimming pool repairs, when the ominous 'out of bounds' sign was frequently displayed, over the years some notable results were achieved. St Martin's continued to enter the Lambeth Schools' and London Schools' galas, and girls gained individual personal survival awards. But, with erratic swimming times, reports showed that the girls 'customary enthusiasm' had waned.

After a week's holiday to recover from taking O levels, fifth-formers embarked on work experience in the community. It started with a two-day conference on Child Care. The group then split up to go to hospitals, schools and nurseries. Daphne Flossman became part of the auxiliary work force in a London teaching hospital, much enjoying the day-to-day, personal contact and even the routine of washing, bed-making and checking temperatures and pulses. The previous year, sixth-form girls had been involved with more long-term assignments, when each Thursday afternoon some had spent time helping at local infant schools and at the Thurlow Park School for Handicapped Children.

Community work continued, but equally necessary was the need to raise money both for charity and school equipment. A sponsored sack-walk by fourth-formers raised £100 for cancer research and a kidney machine, while a sponsored netball-shoot raised £400 for gym equipment which included an international spring-board and various landing mats for both indoor and outdoor use.

During the summer term, Enrichment Courses offered a few 'lucky sixth-formers' opportunities to broaden their understanding of chemistry, history and maths. Twenty-four pupils from different schools, including St Martin's, spent a week studying, evaluating and extracting metals from ore samples, with the Ecton Hill Project at the South London Science Centre in Camberwell. This was combined with lectures and tutorials with notable scientists.

For the history project, a similar group's work was based on the Tower of London, studying mediaeval England. Using special passes, members of the group gained entry to the lecture hall in the education block, where they watched *two and a half films*. 'Two and a half films, as one was so old and worn it was almost impossible to watch,' commented Helen Marsh. A tour of the Tower, lectures and visits to the City Records' Office and the Guildhall Library gave the group material for a final report summarising their busy week.

Three broad areas covered by the Maths Enrichment Course were: Mathematics in Science and the Manipulation of Numbers, How Computers Work and Their Uses, and How We Learn Maths. The final section proved particularly interesting because of showing how secondary school children learn:

'We saw to our amazement how often one child would fall into the same trap time and time again even after being corrected,' wrote Nanita Jain.

Although the enrichment courses came after O level exams, they helped to give a deeper understanding for the following year's A levels.

In the meantime, results of the 1977 exams showed that ninety girls passed from one to eleven O levels, of which thirty had seven or more subjects. Thirty-nine gained A levels, twenty-three went on to university, twelve to other colleges, and one girl won a Schoolgirl Scholarship to America, awarded by the English Speaking Union. But as that summer term ended, another major change in the life of St Martin's was about to begin.

The autumn term started with the usual animated greetings of friends not seen for several weeks, as they caught up with summer holiday activities. There was a feeling of greater importance as they moved up to another year, marking their progress through the school. For new arrivals there was much to learn, and for many it heralded a new system of education in the now non-selective, mini-comprehensive school. The first-year intake also more accurately reflected the multi-cultural society in which St Martin's was set. And soon after the term began, a member of Lewisham Council talked in assembly on Community Relations.

Once again, the busy autumn term was crowded with events including slides showing the school cruise, a film on Invalid Children's Aid and visits to a variety of museums. The upper sixth heard talks from Old Girls on their experiences at different universities and there were outings to the Old Vic and Stratford-upon-Avon. But underlying the familiar came a gradual change as the school faced new challenges.

The curriculum in the first year was broadened, and staff developed a new approach to support girls coming from a much wider background. The question of discipline also had to be reassessed in the fast-moving society of the seventies. Many teachers attended in-service courses, and mingling with the once all-female staff a few male teachers could now be seen.

The rush towards Christmas brought its inevitable build-up, and with it came the sounds of carols being practised in the hall. When the day arrived for the annual carol service at St Martin-in-the-Fields Church, uniforms were checked before everyone climbed into a fleet of coaches for Charing Cross. Here, each form lined up in the church courtyard, waiting to be directed in a long crocodile into the building. But Mrs Wright, starting off the procession, suddenly had to do some quick thinking:

> 'As I led the choir into church,' she said, 'I met Austen Williams declaiming the funeral sentences preceding a coffin. We managed to double back without causing too much stir!'

For the girls waiting outside in chill December, the time seemed endless, before they slowly filed inside to form the main body of the congregation. If the 'down and outs' had come in from the cold, the Reverend Austen Williams always allowed them to sit in the boxes around the pews.

> 'It was quite frightening,' remembered Kate Sidell (née Lister), 'as they were drunk and unruly and used to hurl either themselves or abuse at us.'

But their commotion was soon drowned once the carols rang out.

Because St Martin's was a voluntary-aided church school controlled by governors — thus retaining its individuality and historical links — it was responsible for a certain percentage of the improvement costs, as well as the full cost of maintenance and decorations. In April 1978, a Maintenance and Development Fund was set up to cover the annual contribution paid to the Southwark Diocesan Board, and to help provide improvements to enable St Martin's to develop as an effective small Comprehensive. Parents were asked to contribute regularly, and Old Girls and friends supported the fund too.

Knowledge that Miss Mangold would be leaving, after thirteen years as headmistress, soon filtered through the school. A week before the summer term ended, a leaving party was arranged when a two-part song, composed by sixth-former Alina McGarrigle, was sung to Miss Mangold. In their tribute to her the upper sixth said, 'Miss Mangold knew so well the time and place for authority and used her judgement for our benefit'.

In summing up her own thoughts on her time at St Martin's, Miss Mangold wrote:

'The most notable change was the growth in the size of the sixth form, on both the science and arts sides. As an increasing number of girls went on to university and other forms of higher education, the scope of their subsequent careers widened in consequence. In 1965 it was very difficult for a girl to gain a place in a medical school to train as a doctor; by 1978 it was a reasonable aim for any able applicant. There was a satisfying spread of achievement — psychology, engineering, media studies — and St Martin's girls became students at colleges all over the United Kingdom.'

Also leaving St Martin's at the end of the summer term was Mrs Wright, whose 'unfailing interest, energy and zest' had sustained the music department for nearly twenty years, and her encouragement 'even for the croakiest singers' was remembered:

'Not only did she take a large proportion of the school for class music lessons, but she was responsible for many of the musical items performed on Prize Day and at concerts for the girls and parents. She arranged visits to the Festival Hall and Coliseum Theatre for concerts and operas, and also for the Nucleus Opera Group to perform at school.'

When the autumn term started, with a second intake of mixed ability girls — for which there were three applicants for every place — Miss Ruth How, the deputy head, took over the reins as headmistress. Miss How was no stranger to the school's traditions, having taught physics for many years at St Martin's. 'We were devastated when she stopped teaching us physics just before our O levels,' lamented one Old Girl. Even so, the changeover was smooth, although the school's changing emphasis created its own organisational problems. Miss How was later to write:

'The academic curriculum of a Grammar school was no longer suitable, and in the early days much time was spent in devising a curriculum which would be fitting for a wide ability range. The school remained the same size, which had many advantages but meant that some academic subjects had to be dropped because the school could not afford teachers for very small groups. In those days our expenditure on staff was tightly controlled by ILEA.

'Teachers, many of whom had only taught academic pupils, had to re-think their methods and approach. Help was provided through In-Service training, and with this and the gradual acquisition of teachers with Comprehensive experience we were able to develop the necessary expertise. In time the teaching of pupils with special educational needs became one of the school's strengths.'

This was aided by converting one classroom into a reading centre, where girls with difficulties received extra help.

Another addition was a new home economics block, fully equipped as a furnished flat for house craft, cookery and needlework. And a Quiet Room was created from the old sixth-form cloakroom in the original Silwood building.

Hopes of re-opening the swimming pool were also rekindled, but sadly, after emptying its contents on to the hockey pitch one night, this was not to be. A sponsored swim, planned partly to celebrate the reopening, was quickly changed to a sponsored walk.

On the last Friday afternoon before the October half-term, practically the whole school could be seen walking the perimeter of Brockwell Park. This massive sponsored walk was to raise £1,100 to buy James Allen's low-mileage, three-and-a-half-year-old, fourteen-seater minibus. Several staff undertook the necessary GLC driving test so the minibus could be well used. Later, foam cushions were bought to make the wooden seats more comfortable.

A second sponsored netball-shoot also contributed to the minibus, after high jump stands, badminton posts and much needed hockey equipment had been bought.

At a time when many schools were abandoning uniform, St Martin's frequent uniform checks continued. Tunics for younger girls were phased out so that all girls wore a beige blouse, brown skirt and jersey. With changing fashions, the corduroy Donny Osmond style cap disappeared, and sports shorts were replaced by a short wrap-over pleated skirt over black or brown cycle shorts. For PE, the red Aertex top, on which girls embroidered their names in needlework lessons, continued to be worn.

Discipline was constantly upheld, with detentions meted out most often for, 'Poor behaviour, swearing and taking a day off without good reason,' said Maxine Clarke. Maxine was involved in a dance group outside the school and on one occasion didn't ask permission to be absent from school for the performance. 'I had to do several detentions to make up the time,' she remembered.

Once again, joint Gilbert and Sullivan performances at Alleyn's — this time *The Mikado* — were a riotous success. But sadly for St Martin's there were to be no more, as Alleyn's now had their own girls in all years of the school.

At the Beckenham Festival the first-year choir won the '11 and under' section by one mark. And at the Richmond Festival the junior trio, Lesley Knight, Lih-Ling Wong and Angela Jain, won their class, having 'learned their madrigal in the cloakroom only five minutes before,' wrote sixth-former Tracy Jenkins. 'Moreover they beat the lower sixth. . .which hasn't been forgotten,' Tracy added. The '18s and under' cup was won by Jane Tucker and Sarah Grimwood, with second place gained in most other sections.

The following year, successes were again achieved at Beckenham when the first year and junior choirs won their classes, and Suzy Mico won the Harding Cup for twelves and under. Later in the year, Jane Tucker and Marghanita Potts gained firsts at Richmond, too.

But the success that was achieved in the British Bulgarian Friendship Society's competition was not expected. The competition requirement to sing five songs, two of them in Bulgarian, made winning seem impossible. For the choirs, learning Bulgarian became the 'in-thing'. Even so, some girls had great difficulty with the pronunciation. The problem was solved on the day of the competition by the front row of the choir having the words pinned to their backs, 'to aid the poorer memories in the row behind'. Learning that the choir had won the competition more than made up for all the effort, especially when they heard they would be going to Bulgaria the following March, for an exchange visit with the Secondary English Language School in Plovdiv.

For the less motivated, school was neither popular nor rewarding. Some girls, who had been disenchanted with school when they arrived, perpetuated a chain reaction of disruptive influence, hoping to gain immediate peer status. To avoid further disruptions, wider activities and a more flexible timetable were needed. Banding and setting continued to prevent groups of different abilities holding back the more able, and gave the less able time to consolidate their knowledge. But some girls continued to struggle, although gradually more found motivation in lessons and in the wider variety of school activities.

> 'As a Comprehensive we became primarily a Lambeth neighbourhood school, distinguished from others in the locality by being a Church of England school,' said Miss How. 'Our school community, which had previously been fairly homogeneous, became a stimulating and lively mixture.'

When the first all-ability intake had worked its way up to the fourth year, the curriculum was changed to reflect the broader needs. All classes had English, maths, religious knowledge, PE, careers and 'living', which later became part of Personal, Social and Health Education (PSHE). The remaining subjects were arranged in option blocks, and the choice of one subject from each block had to include at least one science, plus either history or geography or both. This gave a certain flexibility in working towards GCE or CSE exams.

To waste less time moving round the school, the timetable was changed to include six, instead of eight, subjects each day. This also enabled a combined sixth form timetable with Dick Sheppard and Tulse Hill schools, and in 1981 the Trinity Sixth Form Scheme was launched. Twenty-three A level subjects were offered and a greater number of one-year O level and CSE courses. The one-year secretarial course became one of several vocational courses available.

Beyond the school, society was rapidly changing and St Martin's came increasingly to reflect the broader multi-cultural needs of the neighbourhood. The framework of the school remained the same, with its regular core of activities — Founders' Day, the carol service, Prize Day, sports, field trips, museum and theatre visits, concerts, holidays abroad, the old peoples' party, charities and work experience. A termly newsletter now replaced the annual school magazine, but it lost most of the individual contributions from the girls, as the main function was to inform parents of school activities, dates and decisions.

Geography field trip
(School magazine 1981)

In May 1985, the new vicar of St Martin-in-the-Fields Church, Canon Geoffrey Brown, was installed at a service attended by staff and head girls. Canon Brown became a governor of the school, and the following year became chairman, succeeding Prebendary Austen Williams after thirty years in the post.

Computers were now major acquisitions, for the technological age had arrived. Starting with two simple machines, the school gradually added more up-to-date models with the help of the Parents, Staff and Friends Association (PSFA). A network of five computers, with the promise of a sixth to follow, plus the two original machines, formed the basis of the Computer Studies Department. Time spent with word processing, language skills and work leading to exams increased, and to help achieve greater understanding computer clubs met three times a week at break times.

Tuck shops run by girls from each year were set up at break time, too. And once a week in the library gallery Mrs Hore, the librarian, operated a bookshop with pupil helpers. In Bookweek, quizzes and a raffle helped add interest and soon the bookshop was selling stationery and from time to time secondhand books.

'Reading Together', another initiative to create interest in books and reading, encouraged parents and girls to read together at home. As further encouragement, progress certificates for steady effort throughout the year were awarded annually for years one to four.

In the summer of 1985, London Weekend Television organised

an arts festival, when several girls took part in the dance, creative writing and music groups, gaining second and third places in two of the sections. And that term, fifth-former Andrea Coore was selected to perform a solo in the Lambeth Dance Festival.

Another dance activity, staged at the Strand Dance Centre, was attended by the fourth year CSE dance group, who joined nine other groups for an evening of Youth Dance. Practice at the local Youth Dance Workshop at Tulse Hill Youth Centre sustained the interest and attracted many members. The following year a combined PE and dance workshop was held for all second years, with Ujamo, an arts group promoting the Afro-Caribbean approach to dance and music. A report on the workshop said:

> 'They were introduced to songs sung by Ghanaian school children, dances and drumming rhythms. The workshop culminated in a performance by everyone. The atmosphere throughout was one of enjoyment and hard work.'

PE was given a new look when a course of Fitness for Life started a new programme of activities. This included badminton, volleyball, table tennis, trampolining, aerobics, tennis and athletics. And clubs were started for gym, netball, the Duke of Edinburgh's Award and fourth-year dance.

Through all this activity, charities continued to be a major interest, with each form sending a representative to the charities committee. Sponsored walks, runs and spellings all raised money, as well as collections of stamps, milk tops, cans and ring pulls. The Ethiopian appeal figured largely at this time, and each autumn term Crisis at Christmas was supported.

One third form sponsored four-year-old Monika in Mexico, and girls worked hard labelling envelopes, selling cakes, cleaning cars and in a variety of way to raise the necessary sponsorship money. In their fourth year they organised a Mexican evening which included slides, a display, dancing and songs, rounded off by a buffet of Mexican food.

The PSFA was raising money, too, with a jumble sale to buy more computer equipment and headphones for the Modern

Languages Department. And car boot sales were now useful sources of revenue.

During the spring half term of 1986, skiing was again popular when twenty girls and two staff visited Ovronnez, in Switzerland:

'The resort was small but provided good accommodation, food and skiing with a friendly atmosphere,' said a report. 'The pupils were all beginners and by the end of the week most of them had become very proficient, skiing some of the more difficult runs, and gaining their bronze ski-award. Après-ski activities included tobogganing, gluwein tasting, fancy dress, a fondue evening and presentations.'

And the hotel disco was another major attraction.

During the Easter holidays a coach trip was organised to Stratford-upon-Avon to see *Romeo and Juliet*. A group from the fifth and sixth, accompanied by staff and parents, started out at eight in the morning. They returned by eight at night tired but encouraged, for the day's outing had given valuable background for the forthcoming O levels. Other help for O levels came in the form of a photocopier, newly installed in the library.

When the School Council was asked for ways of spending £300 from the School Fund, many ideas were offered. Thirty pounds would provide a Christmas disco, but spending the remainder was open to discussion. Some girls suggested board games such as chess and draughts to use at lunch time. Others thought musical equipment, books for the library, more benches in the grounds or a drinks machine would be useful. Not surprisingly the drinks machine won the vote. However, ILEA was approached to see which firms supplied drinks machines free to schools for a trial period, so the £270 still needed to be spent and more discussion took place.

At the first- and second-year council meeting it was suggested that football should be introduced. With the support and enthusiasm of Bob Smith, a teacher from Dick Sheppard School, this was quickly arranged and soon a number of first to fourth years were involved with the Lambeth Ladies' Football Club.

For several years dissatisfaction had grown, nationally, over the dual examination systems of GCE and CSE, but the autumn term of

1986 heralded a completely new approach to education. Course work, practical skills, oral and written examinations would all give a broader picture of individual achievement through the new General Certificate of Secondary Education (GCSE). Educational criteria for the six examining boards and a monitoring of national standards were also introduced. The seven pass levels of GCSE equated with the former GCE and CSE grades, but allowed more flexibility for different expected levels of attainment.

New subjects were introduced and old ones revamped, with greater integration between subjects. Health education was extended to cover personal and social education (PSHE), and now covered the topics of drugs, smoking and relationships. The Science Department's new technology course for third years was unfolded, starting with the study of fibres and fabrics to show their use in society. This was followed in the spring term with dyes and dyeing, which was linked to Art Department courses.

Part of the learning approach for GCSE courses was to explore broader aspects of each subject. The fourth-year art group was able to appreciate this when they learnt to *read* portraits at the Dulwich Picture Gallery. The following week, a smaller group returned to take part in a video showing the work of the gallery's Education Department. Two of the group were represented at the Young Artists and Designers Exhibition in Kensington Gardens, where the work of fourteen to nineteen-year-olds from ILEA schools and colleges, was displayed to illustrate courses available in art and design.

In music, too, a broader approach was seen when members of the London Sinfonietta came to hear fourth year's compositions, and help them to develop ideas in preparation for a workshop and concert at the Queen Elizabeth Hall. As part of the Young Concertgoers scheme, two members of the London Philharmonic Orchestra also visited the school, to talk to the fourth year option group about life in an orchestra, and in preparation for the group's visit to the Festival Hall for a concert by the LPO.

Snare drums, xylophone and glockenspiel were introduced in music lessons, and girls continued to gain certificates in piano, violin, 'cello, flute, oboe and bassoon. The previous year, twelve girls had been offered places in the London Schools Wind Band. But sadly, when budget cuts were later introduced, charges had to be made for individual lessons, which greatly reduced the number of girls learning to play instruments through the school.

With the absence of Open Evenings for parents, an Any Questions evening was arranged, to answer written questions on education and the day-to-day life of the school. Parents and teachers were concerned about the future direction of the school, because the organisation of secondary education in Lambeth, Southwark and Wandsworth had been under review for many months. Eventually it was announced that:

'There are no plans to amalgamate St Martin's with any other school. It is proposed that school sixth forms will be replaced by Tertiary Colleges in a few years' time; if this happens we shall continue as a small school for girls only of ages 11-16.'

But this decision barely affected St Martin's girls whose immediate interest was far more pressing: rehearsals of *The Wiz*, a rock musical version of *The Wizard of Oz*.

After the performances the newsletter reported:

'The four exhausting nights were a great success with full houses and a lot of enthusiasm from both audiences and cast. . .we are pleased to report that we have received many complimentary comments and letters on the standard of performance and professionalism.'

Over the past two years much building work had been in progress. It had started with the typing room being enlarged, then came the conversion of the former groundsman's cottage into a unit for specialist help for smaller groups of girls. Another newly-completed project was extra heating for the dining room, followed by the removal of asbestos in certain parts of the school. Converting the top floor of the groundsman's cottage into a chapel had also been proposed, and hopes were raised that the whole school would be redecorated in view of its shabby appearance.

A start on the improvements came when new fluorescent lighting was installed throughout the school. Damage caused by the great hurricane in October 1987 meant that a large section of the roof had to be replaced, and sadly the storm also destroyed the ancient mulberry tree, although other damage was comparatively slight. The chapel was completed in December with money donated by the SPCK, through its long association with the school. A further £1,000 for furnishings was raised by the PSFA. Decorating both the inside and outside of the building started a few months later and was to continue for over a year.

In February 1988, thirty-two second years spent five days at the Croft Study Centre in Sussex. A report by Miss Tucker, one of the two members of staff who accompanied them, said:

> 'The weather was cold but pleasant and everyone needed wellington boots after six weeks of almost continuous rain. Most of us managed to get ourselves covered in mud at some stage of the week. The activities included environmental studies at the Croft and in the village of Etchingham as well as brass rubbing in the local church.'

The Battle of Hastings came alive through visiting towns and museums in the area, and the party also studied the magnificent embroidery which traced significant milestones of English history. It was a packed week of historical and environmental interest, and Miss Tucker concluded:

> 'The most memorable activity was a late night walk in the mud, with only four small torches. . .The majority of girls would have done the same thing the next evening, but there were a few who will never visit a wood in the dark again!'

That year saw proposals for a National Curriculum set out in the Education Reform Act (ERA). Described as 'the biggest change to the educational system since 1945', the National Curriculum would introduce staged tests of attainment throughout school life, to show not only what children 'know and understand', but what they can 'create and do'. Having implemented a new national system of exams with the GCSE, all schools would now follow the same subject curriculum, the content being governed by law. And once again, schools began to prepare for the gradual introduction of major changes in the next decade.

In the autumn term, the first effects of the National Curriculum were seen in the Science Department, when Suffolk Co-ordinated Science, a three-year GCSE double science course, was launched for third years. Written work, practical work and all tests would now count towards the, as yet distant, GCSE. The course presented a change of emphasis, but quickly became part of third-year routine.

The valuable work of the PSFA continued to increase with even greater interaction between school and community. One initiative was a stall at the Community Fun Day in Brockwell Park, when £220 was raised. PSFA members spoke to the first years of the work that was being done in raising money for extra amenities. In feedback from the girls, it was again suggested that a selection of indoor games was needed for recreation and lunch breaks.

On another occasion, parents organised sponsored events in the lunch break and a 'Penny Line Day'. A lottery licence was eventually granted so that lotteries and 'grand draws' could be organised on a wider scale. The PSFA ran a Tuck Shop during Arts Festival Week, the culmination of a hectic summer term. The festival included music, drama, sports, 'It's a Knockout', rounders and many activities to round off the busy year.

With the end of the festival came the end of yet another era, for the time had come for Miss How's retirement after seventeen years at St Martin's; eleven as headmistress. In her *School Notes* in the newsletter, Miss How said:

> 'I have been privileged to serve as Headmistress for eleven very interesting and enjoyable years and I have seen the school go through many changes. Now there are stimulating challenges ahead, resulting from the recent Education Act. It is a good time for new leadership, and I am confident that St Martin's will meet the challenges and continue to flourish as a happy and successful school.'

In September 1989, the new headmistress, Miss Anne Philpott, was welcomed to St Martin's.

8. Towards the Future: 1989 - 1999

If the 1980s had seen an acceleration of change, the 1990s were to see still more. Yet, underlying all the changes, St Martin's remained the same to Old Girls returning for the twice yearly OGA meetings. There was the familiar building with its imposing facade. There was the inner hallway below the high domed roof, where countless small girls had sat on the bench anxiously waiting to explain a lateness or misdemeanour to her headmistress.

Even the old laboratories still had the same heavy wooden benches and some of their ancient equipment. The gym, too, looked just as it used to, and peering in, Old Girls saw the wall bars and ropes where once they had climbed and swung. They clattered up the stone stairs at either end of the building, and walked along the green and blue tiled corridors, seeing and remembering so many half-forgotten times. But although Old Girls saw in the past, changes continued to be absorbed within the complex fabric of old and new.

One essential interest that remained constant was an emphasis on reading. A Reading Week was organised with many activities to encourage an interest in books, including half an hour set aside at the end of the afternoon for private reading, 'creating a peaceful end to the day'. At the same time, girls enthusiastically took part in a national *Readathon* for the Malcolm Sargent Fund for Children with Cancer.

Book Boxes for years one to three were set up in the classrooms for independent reading, and reading diaries for short reviews gave a record of books completed. As further encouragement, the Bookshop was opened twice instead of once a week at lunchtime, and more reading weeks were planned when authors would be invited to join in.

Following very successful visits to Luxembourg the previous

year and to Cologne earlier in 1990, the Modern Language Department planned a six-day visit to Strasbourg for the fourth and fifth years' French and German sets. A group of eighteen girls and three teachers set off in the Easter holidays, and Mrs Edwards, the Modern Languages teacher who organised the trip, reported:

> 'We travelled by coach and arrived very early on a wet and stormy Sunday morning to explore the old part of this fascinating and historic town. . . Determined to improve our oral skills, we set out to track down the unwary members of the local population in Strasbourg (for French) — and over the border by bus to Kehl (for German) — submitting them to a barrage of questions.
>
> 'We took time out for one full day excursion into the Vosges mountains where we visited the restored feudal castle of Haut Koenigsbourg and the nearby attractions afforded by a stork park, a monkey mountain and a falconry centre. Other highlights included a visit to one of the local breweries.'

On the way home, the group glimpsed 'the night life of Paris!'

The year before, a group of second and third years had stayed at the Chris Bonington Centre in Cornwall, sailing, raft-making, canoeing, surfing, abseiling and hiking. That year another group took part in environmental studies and outdoor pursuits in North Wales. Both holidays were repeated in subsequent years, and in 1990 third-year Ime Ekong summed up her feelings when she wrote:

> 'The Christian Mountain Centre was an experience of a life-time. I have never in my life been so sick and tired of walking up hills (mountains to me) but I wouldn't have missed it for anything! I had about two hours sleep each night and I still had enough energy to climb up Wales' equivalent of Mt. Everest, go rock-climbing, canoeing and raft-building. . .When people question why I went to the *Christian* Mountain Centre, I will always tell them that the talks we had about the big 'G' were really interesting. Also we all learnt a lot about how to get on with others in all situations. I really enjoyed myself and would love to go again.'

Having joined a mass choir for the musical *African Madonna*, a group of St Martin's girls was invited to perform some of the songs live on *Blue Peter* for One World Week. The impressive occasion was videoed and later shown to the appreciative school governors.

With African interests firmly in mind, a new venture for St Martin's was Black History Month, and in October 1990 a display in the library showed African fabrics, musical instruments, cooking equipment and wood carvings. A competition was held, based around the display and new library books on African history. Every year a different country's history and culture would be explored in a similar way, giving a true feeling of the background and individual development.

Technology had become increasingly important, and that autumn term the new National Curriculum technology course was started for the first years. The English Department also took advantage of Information Technology (IT), when time was allotted to use the school's two networks. The impressive array of computers was quickly mastered and girls edited their work on screen, creating a far more finished end-product. 'Somehow the screen made them more aware of their mistakes!' was a wry comment.

Another initiative, introduced with the National Curriculum, was the changed system of form classification. To follow on from primary schools, which ran from Year 1 to Year 6, secondary schools now started at Year 7. Year 11 was the final year at St Martin's and equivalent to the fifth form, because sixth-form colleges and colleges of further education catered for those who went on to take A levels, B Tec or similar courses. Later came a more integrated assessment for National Vocational Qualifications (NVQs).

Year numbering was now linked to four Key Stages, with assessment at the end of each one. Primary schools were to cover Key Stages 1 and 2, and secondary schools Key Stage 3 for Years 7, 8 and 9, and Key Stage 4 for Years 10 and 11.

Parents were to have greater involvement, too, with information and assessment results freely available under a system of 'Reporting Back'. They were advised on the homework policy and the importance attached to making sure all homework was completed. And pupils' own self-evaluation would indicate their overall confidence and their attitude to subjects. As a link between home and school, St Martin's girls each had a Day Book, where reasons for absence also had to be recorded. All this extra assessment and form 'business' added considerably to the workload of the staff, and parents' co-operation was vital.

In the busy autumn term of 1990, a second Reading Week took place, and another *Readathon*. For girls studying child development, a successful visit to the Museum of Childhood in Bethnal Green showed the history and popularity of toys, and resulted in a variety of toys being made in school. A fashion show at the Assembly Rooms, Lambeth, enabled another group to model forties, fifties and sixties fashions as part of the Lambeth Age Concern's fiftieth celebrations. And girls ventured to the new Camberwell Choir School on Saturdays.

When sixty girls took part in an instrumental concert in the school hall, Mrs Zimmerman, Head of Music, said:

> 'There was a large appreciative audience and the instrumentalists and singers performed confidently, competently and professionally! Music presented ranged from one of the oldest pieces of written music, "Summer is a-coming in" to pieces written by performers. The evening reflected many hours of careful practice from pupils and inspired teaching from the peripatetic staff.'

For several years, interest in steel drums had been growing, and opportunity had been given for girls to visit a local music centre to practise. But the addition of the school's own steel pans greatly enriched the music classes with their lively rhythm. Two girls joined the London Youth Steel Orchestra, which gave a performance at St Martin's and later went on a tour of Italy.

Piano and violin lessons may have seemed less adventurous by comparison; even so, girls continued to take exams and study the theory of music. In the spring term of 1991, Melissa Gaynair and Phyllis Pearce 'boldly demonstrated their skills on the violin' in a workshop held for the top classes of St Jude's Primary School, Herne Hill. Over the years, the musical tradition had continued with visits to concerts, opera and jazz, as well as many opportunities for the choir to perform.

Wider interests were beginning to encourage the less-motivated, but Miss Philpott was convinced that all the girls at St Martin's could and should do better. She held 'brain-storming' sessions with her deputies and senior staff, to try to work out a dynamic approach that would enthuse the whole school. 'Facilities raise morale,' Miss Philpott said, but the dedication of the staff and belief that standards *could* be raised were vital too. Above all, it was important to create a happy working environment in which the girls believed in their ability to achieve more, thus developing a pride in themselves and the school.

School rules and a code of conduct were important, and these were explicitly set out so that pupils and parents could sign their agreement to them. They included the strict standards of behaviour, uniform and homework which were constantly enforced.

Although many girls were classed as 'disadvantaged', the positive attitude of Miss Philpott and her staff engendered enthusiasm. Much encouragement, rewards, certificates for achievement, extra-curricula activities and after-school study sessions all helped to cement this positive approach. Special-needs staff worked from the Learning Development Department. But it was explained that *all* students are special and all have needs, most being met within the mainstream setting.

Particular needs were noted when prospective students in Year 6 were visited in their primary schools. Once at St Martin's, a Day Sheet accompanied each Year 7 class and was returned to the form teachers who collated the information. In this way special needs would more quickly be identified.

A well-illustrated, re-designed brochure set out the aims, brief history and traditions of the school, and stated:

> 'St Martin's provides a rich and varied educational experience for each of its pupils, encouraging their full development and equipping them for life and work in the 21st century.'

Girls' views were also expressed and on leaving school one Year 11 pupil said:

> 'St Martin's has been a great school. Its foundation has enabled me to achieve the best of everything and mature from a school girl to an adult.'

By the summer term of 1991, a multi-media workshop had been established with a variety of audio cassette players and head-phones, a television, video and a growing number of books. Many companies had responded to an appeal earlier in the year by donating money and equipment, and several volunteers spent time putting material on tape. Blank tapes were constantly needed and many were donated. In addition to use by classes and small groups, tapes were enjoyed at break and lunch times.

As interest grew so more space was needed, and soon work began on larger premises for the workshop. A grant of £200, donated by the Notley Foundation in San Marino, California, greatly helped towards the renovations. The first CD Rom arrived in the autumn term, with software for an atlas and an encyclopaedia. But more advanced material and a dictionary were soon to follow.

As part of the GCSE Business Studies course, Year 11 girls had to present a viable study of 'Business Research and Promotion'. First a gap needed to be identified in the market — the school environment — then, working in groups, mini enterprises were set up and run for two weeks. Many intriguing gaps were filled as girls established their businesses, promoting sales of shares, keeping careful records and finally distributing profits to shareholders and a variety of charities.

Scrunchies, a successful hairband business, was set up by one group of girls. McMartins Snackbar partnership was organised by another, with stiff competition from St Martin's Tuck Shop. A jewellery shop and Classic Fragrance also gave essential business experience and showed the need to work as a team. The following year, Miss Muscles Car Valeting Service ran a sales-promotional prize draw, while Yum Yums Tuck Shop and the Lunchbox plc both did brisk business. These were busy and rewarding times, not just for the girls taking part, but for all who were cajoled into supporting the different enterprises.

An interest in woodwind instruments had led to the school's woodwind players attending a workshop at the Centre for Young Musicians. As a result a new lunchtime wind band had been formed. In the spring of 1993, enthusiasm was encouraged when Mr Ibsen, a keen singer and horn player, temporarily took over class music. He arranged starter courses in brass instruments, and girls were able to contribute to an instrumental concert at the end of the term.

A collection of telephones, brought to the school by the Design Council's education officer, formed the basis of an investigation by Year 8, who studied the way in which telephones had developed since the 1930s. Afterwards, girls designed their own phones using a variety of materials, and their work was displayed at the Design Council in The Haymarket. It later became part of an article in the magazine *Designing*.

Key Stage assessments, called Standard Assessment Tasks (SATs), took place for Year 9 in the summer term of 1993. Written tests in English, mathematics, science and technology started in June, although pilot tests had been run the previous year for maths and science. Teachers' assessment of work carried out in lessons would then be combined with results of the SATs to give an overall National Curriculum level. All schools' internal assessments had to be checked by outside moderation, so results were not expected until the autumn term.

A major issue for 1993 was opting for Grant Maintained status. Earlier in the year many discussions had taken place, and ballot forms were sent to parents to glean their opinions. Following the result of the ballot, an application was submitted to the Secretary of State for Education, and the school waited to hear whether it had been successful. In July, after many anxious moments, it was announced that GM status had been achieved, starting from the 1st of September.

The first consideration was to prepare a bid for a capital grant to create a new Technology Centre, and a 'splendid document complete with colour photographs of the girls at work in Technology lessons' was submitted. The result of the bid would take many months to come through, so the school waited once more, this time to see whether funds would be provided to convert the long-disused swimming pool into a new hive of activity.

The National Curriculum stated that in outdoor and adventurous activities 'pupils should share experience with others, often in difficult, unfamiliar and challenging environments'. With this aim in

The disused swimming pool (Siddall)

mind, forty-six girls from Year 8 took part in a 'super adventure break' at the Manor Adventure Centre in Shropshire. Rosemary Lewis reported:

> 'When we arrived, we collected our baggage and we were shown to our rooms by an instructor. Our Instructor told us the rules for the room. We made our beds and put our things in the proper place. . . During the week we did activities and exercises. Most of the activities were scary — and excellent! We did highropes, night walks, abseiling, bike riding and lots more. Towards the end of the week, different groups had the opportunity to go into town to buy presents and souvenirs for their family and friends. The majority enjoyed their week and would like to say to their parents, "That was money well spent!".'

For many years, St Martin's had been divided into lower, middle and upper sections, but with the Key Stage system firmly established it became more appropriate to use Key Stage 3 and Key Stage 4 as natural divisions. Each Key Stage had its own director and deputy, but it was emphasised that the first point of contact from home should be the form teacher, and then the Key Stage directors.

Repeated reminders about school uniform, with no jewellery, had kept up a high standard. Miss Philpott reported that many compliments were received from people outside the school, including parents of prospective pupils. It was emphasised that the girls' smart appearance continued to make a valuable contribution to the positive image of the school. Even so, outdoor coats, and shoes as stated on the uniform list — not trainers, trainer-type shoes or boots — sometimes caused problems. But having praised parents and pupils who took pride in the uniform, Miss Philpott announced:

> 'Any girl arriving at school who is not wearing full school uniform will be sent home to change immediately.'

This was no idle threat. On the first morning after the announcement, girls who arrived in a motley assortment of clothes were sent home to change. Staff waited anxiously to see what would happen, but within an hour the girls returned smartly dressed in full uniform.

Now, uniform reminders in the newsletter became less frequent, apart from announcing simple changes. One such change was the introduction of a red jumper with a brown neck stripe for years nine, ten and eleven, to replace the brown with red stripe which younger girls continued to wear.

The only concessions to strict uniform enforcement were on special 'non-uniform days', which had crept into schools across the country as a way of raising money for particular charities. The PSFA sometimes organised non-uniform days, and on one occasion girls were asked to bring in items of bric-à-brac, to be sold at car boot sales to provide a further source of money for much needed equipment for the school.

Other good causes were not forgotten, and over the years money was regularly raised for the British Legion Poppy Appeal, St Martin-in-the-Fields Church Social Care Unit, Crisis at Christmas, Children in Need and many more appeals and charities. Year 10 raised money for a children's hospice in Oxford, initially by selling Christmas cards and decorations and later by organising an entertainment. They intended to keep up their commitment until they were no longer at St Martin's.

The Magic of Communications was the title of an intriguing lecture given at the Barbican Centre in February 1994. To the Year

10 science group it was no ordinary lecture, as Sarah Still and Karen Picken pointed out:

> 'The lights began to dim and there was a hushed silence throughout the schools that were sitting in the hall. To our amazement there was then a huge display of flashing lights on the stage and a gigantic television screen that was suspended in the air at the back of the stage lit up with a computerised visual reality image of a man's face.
>
> 'The lecture contained information about the telephone, the electromagnetic spectrum and waves, optical fibre communications, radio systems and satellites, analogue and digital systems, switching and relays, networks, services and terminals, telling us the history and present developments in communications...'

The audience was involved as far as possible, and a St Martin's girl was one of three volunteers who was chosen to help with the experiments.

Back at school, communications were enhanced when a cheque for £900 from the PSFA enabled a portable public address system to be bought. Remaining money from the cheque bought books for the library, and more books were bought with money sent from an Old Girl living in Canada, in appreciation for her 'St Martin's education'.

Early in 1994 girls had clapped in Assembly when Miss Philpott announced that both areas of washbasins and lavatories were to be completely modernised. The inevitable noise, dust and disruption that followed, while the builders were at work, were amicably tolerated, because there had been problems with the plumbing for many years. The issue had frequently cropped up at School Council meetings, when form representatives discussed both minor and major resolutions.

One particularly important discussion that took place was the school's policy on bullying and verbal abuse. The increase in bullying in schools all over the country was causing alarm, and individual schools began constructing a definite policy to curb it. At St Martin's, an anti-bullying charter was devised to be presented to each form at the start of the autumn term.

Other points discussed by the School Council were suggestions for healthy eating through the school's meal service, and the monthly focus on international dishes. Deputy head, Mrs Morrison, in commenting on the work of the Council, said:

'The representatives have been articulate and forthright, with many sensible ideas about making St Martin's an even more cohesive, harmonious community.'

Several visits to France were organised by the Modern Languages Department in 1994, and February had seen Year 9 pupils enjoying a weekend in Boulogne. The following month, forty-seven Year 8 girls went to Boulogne for the day. A weekend visit to Paris for Year 9 was organised in July, and with many opportunities for practising French and mixing with young people, the Modern Languages Department intended making visits to France a regular feature of the curriculum.

Ecoutez, a French club in the school's library for Years 7 and 8, was another popular way of helping master the French language, and members were able to borrow cassettes and books to practise their French at home. A visit to the Eurotunnel Exhibition showed Year 7 girls how the tunnel was being constructed. Afterwards, Cassandra Williams commented:

'All the building work for the Eurotunnel does look ugly, but if you think about it there will be no delays due to bad weather.'

The exhibition brought France a little nearer, as girls learnt how both sides of the tunnel were being constructed.

In the on-rush of the technological age, physical education was not neglected, and in June girls from Years 7 and 8 represented St Martin's at the Lambeth Schools Athletic Competition. Of the seven schools that took part, St Martin's gained second place. Three of the winners in their sections went on to represent Lambeth in the London Championships and came first in their events. Rosemarie Lewis, the discus winner for Year 8, said:

'I felt good (and shocked) when they said I had come first. I couldn't believe it. I didn't think I would actually win. I was very proud that I had won for my school, St Martin's, the whole of London Athletic Championships.'

Antoinette Wong, also in Year 8, was overwhelmed when she was selected for the Lambeth Championships and realised she had a lot of training to do before the event. However:

> 'When the race started, I knew what I had to do — just keep running as fast as I could until I reached the finishing line. I already had experience from previous races which were not as important as this race. When I knew I had won, I was really surprised because I thought my friend was going to beat me. I would like to thank everyone in the PE Department for their support.'

After being selected for the London championship, Antoinette went still further and reached the semi-finals in the English Schools Championships.

On Tuesday the 22nd of November 1994, governors, staff, pupils, architects and builders came together to mark the start of work to build the new Technology Centre. The bid had been successful! But instead of converting the disused swimming pool, as had originally been suggested, land previously bought adjacent to Holy Trinity Church was considered a more suitable site. Lady Reid, the chair of the governors, performed the 'turning the sod' ceremony.

The new centre would incorporate rooms for wood, metal and plastic, a textiles room, a 'food' room, preparation and store rooms and a department office. Deputy head Mrs Morrison, complete in yellow hard hat, became Project Manager to oversee the work which was due to be completed by the following September. Meanwhile, girls watched the once rough ground gradually being transformed.

In January, visits were arranged to see *Grease* at the Dominion Theatre for Year 8, and *The Merchant of Venice* at the Bloomsbury Theatre for Year 10. Year 10 also visited the Royal Albert Hall to hear *Making Waves*, a lecture on the discovery of electromagnetic induction. Aisha Brown gave a report of the outing and after describing their eventful journey said:

> 'The building was spectacular. The lighting on the stage had a strong effect on us and the rest of the audience. . .In the lecture we learnt how Faraday invented a continuous electrical current and how he invented the first telephone. Also we learnt how war time veterans were able to communicate with their ships for the first time. Next came a talk about mobile phones and how they are constructed. The lecturer predicted that everyone will be using a mobile phone by the year two thousand, if we can afford it!'

Comic Relief created a week on the lighter side, yet one of considerable hard work. Throughout the country, Comic Relief had become established as a light-hearted way of raising money for international relief, and St Martin's played its part.

Individual girls, forms and staff organised sponsored events, cleaned shoes, washed cars, sold food and ran raffles. Some pupils dressed up, and some teachers wore school uniform. Mrs Morrison was even hosed down with cold water — all in an effort to raise money. A Comic Relief representative spoke in assembly, explaining how the money was used, and at the end of the week over £500 had been raised with more still to come.

A prestigious distinction in 1995 was gained by Kelly Shine, in Year 10, who received a Young Citizen of the Year Award. It was presented to her by a television actress from *The Bill*, which much enhanced the occasion.

More winners, this time for a design competition, were Karen Picken, Sarah Still and Melissa Thomas. The previous year, Year 10 textiles group had been given the brief to design a new cover for the grand piano in the hall. The group worked hard in their textiles lessons and the final, winning design incorporated the school's crest of St Martin and the beggar.

An outing to Mitcham Common to study woodland, grassland and pond habitats was enjoyed in the summer term by a group from Year 7. They identified many different trees, birds, animals and insects, and their report concluded:

> 'We also went pond dipping in Seven Islands Pond. We found various animals including dragon flies, damsel flies and minnows. There were many bugs in the water like whirlygig beetles, water fleas and pond skaters. We had a great afternoon. Finally, thank you to everyone who helped to organise our trip.'

For Year 10, their outing to Dartford was unusual but equally interesting.

The group visited the Littlebrook D Power Station where they watched a video showing the work of the power station, before donning hard hats to be taken on a conducted tour to see the awe-inspiring complexity of massive machinery. For the previous three years, geography outings had been to Bewl Water reservoir, near Lamberhurst, Kent, and both centres gave ample fieldwork opportunities for GCSE.

Year 9 celebrated Women in Science and Engineering Day by attending workshops at school run by twelve women in scientific fields. By explaining their own first-hand experiences, the visitors helped girls explore some of the careers in science and engineering open to women. The visit was much enjoyed by girls and visitors, and was to be repeated by other 'women in science' in subsequent years.

The day finally arrived when the new Technology Centre was ready. The building, rising slowly over the past eight months, had been a source of great interest. With finishing touches completed, the technology staff busily transferred equipment from its old home to the brand new building. New equipment, financed by further grants and donations, was set in place ready for the start of the autumn term.

But the builders did not leave St Martin's because further improvements were planned. Two former technology rooms were to be converted for the Art Department, and a new science laboratory was created to accommodate a larger intake of girls that was moving up the school. The kitchen, which was described as 'positively antique', also needed major refurbishments, so building work continued.

To make sure all National Curriculum subjects had a fair allocation of time, the timetable was restructured to allow forty instead of thirty lessons a week. Registration was at 8.40, followed by assembly as usual. Then came six lessons interspersed by Recreation (Rec) at 10.15. with the catering service available in the dining hall, and a further five-minute changeover time at 11.50. Lunch was between 1 and 2 o'clock, when a second registration took place, although only Year 11 girls were allowed to leave the premises during the lunch hour. Two more lessons followed, with school ending at 3.30. Precision timing was needed, especially in moving from one area to another.

In September, 1995, the Reverend Nicholas Holtam became vicar of St Martin-in-the-Fields Church, taking over from Canon Brown after his retirement. The Reverend Holtam became a vice chairman of the school governors with the General Secretary of the SPCK, Mr Paul Chandler, who kept up the SPCK's ancient connection with the school.

October had become a time for celebrating poetry, through National Poetry Day. In helping to create an awareness of the pleasures of poetry, poetry reading sessions were held at lunch time, when girls visited the library to read or listen to many different poems.

Because of the enormous increase in traffic, the fleet of coaches no longer travelled up to Trafalgar Square for the annual carol service. Founders' Day would continue to be held in London, but carols were practised ready for a local carol service at St Paul's, Trinity Rise.

The noise of builders and building continued through the autumn term and into the new year, with inevitable disruptions at lunch time, but the catering manager, Mrs Margaret Marchant, promised that the girls would be fed regardless. More plans were now being discussed for the derelict swimming pool — once the focus for so many girls. This time a dance and drama studio was to be the aim.

A new venture for the Art Department was a four-day trip to Paris, in the bitterly cold February of 1996. Mrs Davies, Head of Art, said:

> 'We broke the journey from Calais to Paris with a short trip to see some First World War trenches. We had the advantage of a very knowledgeable guide. His commentary, and the fact that it was snowing and very muddy, gave us all an insight into the conditions which the soldiers had to endure. Those girls studying History found the visit particularly interesting.'

The busy four days were crowded with visits to the Louvre, the Pompidou Centre, the Orangerie and the Musée d'Orsay, where different artistic styles were amply displayed. The girls 'took it all in their stride and were never short of comments — complementary or otherwise!'

During the Easter holidays, GCSE Revision Courses were held for Year 11. From 9.30 to 1pm, fifteen members of staff organised and supervised the various sections. Attendance was good and remained steady throughout the four days, as girls brushed up their studies ready for their forthcoming exams. Because of its success and obvious benefit, Mrs Constantinou, deputy head of the English Department and course organiser, planned repeat courses for future Year 11 students.

Welcome news greeted the girls when they returned for the summer term to find the newly-refurbished kitchen fully operational. The importance of a good midday meal was stressed, and that with the wide choice of hot and cold meals girls should choose something other than 'just chips', preferably the excellent-value, two-course meal. There were 'healthy options', too, including vegetarian dishes, salads, fresh fruit and yogurts.

The Equal Opportunities Group, together with a self-help group concerned with the educational attainment of inner-city children, organised weekly discussions for Years 9 and 10. The previous year, through TVEI funding, a similarly successful group had taken place. It was hoped that through discussion, girls would examine topical issues, further develop self-esteem and be guided towards higher educational goals. In summing up her feelings, Kelly Coberne from Year 10 said:

'I found the discussion group extremely useful. It gave me an insight into many careers I knew nothing about, as well as stressing the importance of education. Not only did the discussion group assist me educationally but also socially. I met a range of people that I was unfamiliar with and by the time the discussion group was over, I felt I knew them a little better.'

Disability Awareness Week was a new concern for the school. The aims were 'to raise the understanding of difficulties faced by disabled people, to discourage negative attitudes and to learn about the positive ways in which the disabled contribute to society'. Various money-raising events were arranged by the girls, and Natalie Walters from Year 7 said:

'I did a sponsored silence to raise money for charity. It was hard because people were trying to get me to talk, but I did it in the end. I raised £9.60. The sponsored silence made me realise that life is not easy for the deaf and people who can't speak.'

Through the week, several visiting speakers explained how the Disability Awareness aims were being achieved. And one visitor, a blind musician, sang and played to the school.

That summer term, of 1996, proved to be another milestone in the history of the school, because St Martin's was granted technology college status. This latest development had been achieved because of a partnership forged with Accord Energy, who had provided funding to create a new Business Studies and IT Centre. As well as greatly improving the business studies facilities, a further thirty-station network was installed which would benefit girls throughout the school. With the status of a technology college, additional funding was also available to refurbish a further two science laboratories and provide a resource area for the Mathematics Department.

The new Business Studies and IT Centre was due to be ready in the autumn term, and work on the improvements carried on through the summer holidays. But this emphasis on technology did not exclude other areas, for at the same time the Victorian coach house in the school grounds was transformed into a modern music centre. Candice Greene, in Year 7, described her feelings when the Music Centre was opened:

'When I first stepped into the new room it smelt fresh, I can't explain it, a kind of polishy, painty smell. It also smelt of new instruments.'

And Victoria Northey, also from Year 7, said:

'I think that music is really good; it's even better in the new music block. We have new equipment and an excellent teacher called Miss Meardon. . . We also have a quiet room where we can practise in peace.'

Interest in music had increased, not least by the steel pan groups, some of whose members practised after school with a group of players in Brixton, organised by music teacher, Mr Rollock. Under his guidance, girls from Years 10 and 11 combined to record a tape of their music at a local recording studio. Copies of the tape were sold to provide much needed funds to complete a new set of steel pans.

When thirty CDs were given to the Music Department by Mrs Boreham, Head of Religious Studies, these greatly increased the variety of music for GCSE students. The group gained further encouragement when they formed part of the audience at the Royal Academy of Music, for the Piano Masterclass which was broadcast in the BBC Young Musician of the Year series. Later, GCSE groups joined workshops organised by the Camberwell Choir School, and seven St Martin's girls took part in the concert that followed.

The school's gospel choirs had come into existence partly due to popular request. First came the senior choir made up from the GCSE music group, whose members were asked to sing at the Farriers' carol service in the City. This then became an annual event, and in the meantime many further requests for the choir were made. Three members responded to requests from girls in Year 9 to help set up their own choir, and both Years performed at the Year 11 leaving celebrations. 'The resulting performance can only be described as spectacular,' commented Miss Meardon, the new Head of Music.

Year 8 also wanted their own choir, so four girls from Year 11 undertook to train them. That left Year 7, who quickly followed enthusiastically with a choir, too. Professional training was now given at school, and their singing talent was put to the test at a Choirs by Candlelight concert at St Martin-in-the-Fields Church. For Year 7 this was their first public performance, and their confidence and singing ability gave no hint of the short while they had been together.

Miss Meardon reported:

> 'The Gospel Choirs continue to go from strength to strength under the wonderful guidance of Danny Thomas. Numbers are growing at the lunch time rehearsals, and the hard work is paying off.'

Another exciting event for the Music Department came when the Year 9 choir won the Royal Mail/Choice FM gospel choir competition, which was later broadcast on Christmas Day. The £1,000 prize money the school received paid for full-length, red gowns for the choir, and these added a professional dignity to their performances.

Much was happening in the art world, too. On a gloriously sunny September day, Year 11 visited Kew Gardens where time was spent drawing, taking notes and photographs, in preparation for their first unit of work on plant structures. Year 10 visited the Tate Gallery to learn more about twentieth century art, which complemented their focus on 'abstraction'. And much 'exciting and interesting sketch-book work' resulted from a visit to the British Museum by the whole of Year 7. At the same time, this visit enabled the girls to develop research skills and deepen their knowledge of the Ancient Egyptians.

A business link-up, which was established earlier in 1996, enabled the Year 10 business studies class to visit Marks and Spencer in Oxford Street. This was part of the 'In Company with Schools' project which created the link. Before the visit, preparation work gave an insight into the organisation, its structure and person-nel department. In a report of their visit, Emma Taylor and Caroline May said:

> 'When the day finally arrived, we met at Brixton and arrived at the Pantheon Store, Oxford Circus, at 10.10am. We checked in and were issued with security passes and swipe cards. We used our swipe cards (cards which enabled us to enter locked doors backstage) and saw a huge lift which con-tinually moved. We were shown how to enter the lift safely and we discov-ered how difficult it was to jump in as it passed.'

During the day girls were assigned to members of staff in different departments, to learn the varied jobs and pressures involved.

> 'We had a really enjoyable day,' they agreed, 'and wished we had been able to stay longer, but we knew what hard work was coming next — to write up our work and make a presentation.'

The presentations were later given not only to their year and mem-bers of staff, but also to three representatives from Marks and Spencer and two Ofsted inspectors. Content, style and delivery were judged and comments made on individual members of each group. Emma and Caroline admitted that everyone was nervous, but added that they had enjoyed their first big presentation and that the visitors had given positive feedback.

The inclusion of Ofsted inspectors was because of the school inspection that took place at the end of October. Earlier in the term an evening meeting had been arranged for parents, when they had put their points of view and assessment of the school. The Ofsted inspectors then spent a busy four days examining all aspects of the school as part of the four-yearly report.

'I was very touched,' said Miss Philpott, 'when two separate groups of girls, being interviewed by Ofsted inspectors, described the school as being like a family.'

After-school Spanish lessons were introduced that autumn, for a group of Year 10 girls and two members of staff. They started working towards the GCSE exam which they hoped to take after two years' study. To help perfect their Spanish accent, they chatted to members of the domestic staff who came from Spanish-speaking countries of South America.

Another language interest was found in the Latin Club. The club had started two years earlier, again for Year 10s and some teachers, and was held in the Cottage at lunch times. When it was introduced, English teacher the Reverend Duncan Crawford had said:

'The course aims to complement our English language work, to provide etymological and grammatical background and to build up vocabulary.'

In the Spring of 1997 a new Latin course took place through the Latin Club, and Nadia Khan and Sarah Crawford described the meetings:

'Each session lasted an hour and during this time we learnt the relationship between the Latin language and our own modern language which we use today. Each of us participated in reading in Latin to the rest of the class. . . All of us who attended the club really enjoyed it.'

The sessions continued for twelve weeks, and for the last occasion Mrs Marshall, the catering manager, prepared various dishes which 'might have been eaten two thousand years ago when Latin was spoken,' said Nadia and Sarah.

With increasing activities old, familiar ones were not forgotten, as groups of girls continued to work for their Duke of Edinburgh awards, gaining valuable experience in life-skills. Field trips and visits to London's major museums and exhibitions all took place each term. New parents visited the school with their daughters to see the school in action. And all the while the new interlinked computer networks were being used from 8am to 5pm each day.

Work experience continued with a preparation day, which included mock interviews, presentations, discussions and workshops run by employers and consultants in different fields. This was followed by one-day placements for Year 10 girls, to give a brief taste of first-hand experience in different types of work. After completing two weeks' work experience, each girl was given a certificate and an employer's report which were added to her National Record of Achievement (NRA) folder.

For Year 9, guidance was given by a senior careers advisor for South Bank Careers. Four seminars were held for pupils and parents, to show what options and qualifications were available at St Martin's and beyond. International Women's Week was celebrated each year, too, when the positive contributions that women had made, and were making, were explored through displays and in assembly.

In the summer term, sixty girls from St Martin's took part in the Lambeth Schools Athletics Championships, held at Tooting Bec Athletics Stadium. Four went on to represent Lambeth at the London Schools Athletics Championships, and Anisha Barnaby became one of fifty who were selected to represent London in the English Schools Championships, where she came fifth in the 200m race.

The 5-a-side football team was gaining trophies, too. In a seven-schools tournament St Martin's came third, and Lisa Thomson from Year 8 was presented with a trophy for 'best player of the match'. St Martin's team went on to play football in Croatia, and Lisa reported:

'It was one of the most interesting places I have ever visited. The people were extremely kind. Out of the teams we came 4th. The women we played were often much older than us, nevertheless the team came back with five trophies.'

That year, the annual sports day proved to be the only dry day of the week. The sun shone and there was a slight breeze as girls 'ran fast, jumped high and far and threw implements a great distance'. There was also a tug-of-war where teams pulled with determined enthusiasm.

But one of the greatest and most prestigious events of 1997 was the success of the gospel choir. Having perfected their performance through regional qualifying rounds, many accomplished choirs came together for the finals of the National Festival of Music for Youth at the Queen Elizabeth Hall on the South Bank. Once again, St Martin's 'stunned the audience' with their rendering of *Something Inside So Strong*, and even the adjudicators admitted to being in tears.

Afterwards, a Welsh choir, who gave an equally fine performance, described St Martin's singing as *magnificent*. Credit was due to the hard work of the girls, Miss Meardon Head of Music, and to the musical director Danny Thomas who 'constantly interrupted his international career to train them'. The whole school was proud to learn that the choir was presented with the National Festival of Music for Youth's Outstanding Performance Award.

As a result, the senior choir was later invited to perform at the Schools Prom in the Royal Albert Hall. Later still, the same choir was to take part in the 750th anniversary service of the Bethlem Royal Hospital, in St Paul's Cathedral. Another performance was to be in November to celebrate St Martin's Day, and recorded for Channel Five as part of a lunchtime concert at St Martin-in-the-Fields Church. Individual and joint engagements continued, which gave great satisfaction to the girls who took part, and honour to the school, as well as enjoyment to many audiences.

Encouragement for the English Department came when links were established with the Young Vic Theatre. As part of their Schools Theatre Festival, a group from Year 9 worked on Arthur Miller's *A View From the Bridge*, a GCSE text, and performed an improvised piece based on the play. Another theatre link was forged when St Martin's became one of nine successful schools to take part in the Royal National Theatre Stage Door Schools Project. With this partnership, an artist-in-residence would provide drama workshops.

Subsidised tickets for various performances and backstage tours of the Royal National Theatre also resulted.

CD Roms, now a feature of the library as well as the Technology Centre, helped too. The wide range of titles was constantly booked at lunchtimes and after school to support coursework. Kelly Burns in Year 9 wrote:

> 'I used the *Romeo and Juliet* disc for my English SATs revision. I looked at the "characters" part and read about Romeo and watched video clips from the play. I think the CD Rom really helped me to understand the play and to do well in my exams.'

Part of the school library (School archives)

A new slant on dramatic interpretation came with the introduction of Theatre Active. This was run by teacher-actors who worked with groups of pupils on aspects of their personal and social development. Guided by the theatre company director, Year 8 explored situations where disputes might lead to conflict. The ideas were then used in the PSHE lessons to explore the consequences of the decisions reached in the acting sessions.

National Bookweek had become another welcome change from routine, when each day Years 7, 8 and 9 read their own chosen book during the last afternoon session. A competition to design a book cover or a poster advertising a favourite book created further interest, and book reviews and letters to authors were written. A visit from a popular author, who led lively discussions and explained writing techniques, added to the diversity of Bookweek.

Earlier in the year poetry had not been forgotten, when the English Department organised a Celebration of Poetry. The Year 7 forms took part in either individual or group presentations of their favourite poems. Certificates were awarded and the best form was presented with the English Cup.

Miss Philpott's belief that St Martin's girls could and should do better, and the strategies that followed, had reaped rewards. In successive years the percentage of girls gaining five or more GCSE grades A-C had risen from 18% in 1994 to 35% in 1997. These were described as 'remarkable results', especially when set against the statistic that nearly half the pupils were classified as having special needs, with 3.5% requiring a formal statement.

In an interview with the *Church Times*, Miss Philpott said that success could not have been achieved without the commitment of the staff, who organised after-school study sessions, Saturday morning courses and Easter GCSE revision courses. Enthusing the girls with confidence in their ability had been another key strategy. The report concluded by expressing the school's aim of continuing to increase the percentage of five or more GCSE passes in the coming years.

Towards the end of 1997, underpinning the front of the old school building once more had to be undertaken and caused much mud and disruption. Miss Philpott commented:

> 'If you have seen St Martin's recently you will have seen the mud and trenches which make the front of our lovely old house, Silwood, look rather like the battlefields of the Somme during the First World War!. . .Visitors are having to use the porch doors and be guided to Reception by members of Year 8, who are doing a wonderful job.'

By contrast, the majority of the classrooms had undergone attractive redecorations in a 'warm peach colour', and the ancient heating system had been overhauled. Closed circuit TV cameras had also been installed, and a high security fence was planned, both as a result of a government grant for improved school security.

February saw yet another science lab refurbished, much to the delight of staff and girls alike. One Year 9 pupil, who described the improved laboratories as 'a real privilege to work in' added, 'They are pleasant and roomy and provide a proper working environment.'

The science labs were made available to children from St Jude's Primary School, Herne Hill, and after their visit, in the spring term of 1998, Tobias Allman wrote:

> 'It was a great pleasure joining you in your workshop. We really did enjoy it. I really like Science and so you helped me even more to understand what Science is all about. I am writing just to say that we appreciate your invitation. . . I really enjoyed answering the questions you gave us to do on the laptop computer. But my best part was using the test-tubes.'

When the gospel choir received an invitation from the SPCK to sing at a service to celebrate the 300th anniversary of their founding, the honour was felt by the whole school. Lady Reid, Miss Philpott and her two deputies also attended the occasion in St Martin-in-the-Fields Church, where the service was taken by the Reverend Nicholas Holtam. The Queen, as patron of the Society, was accompanied by the Duke of Edinburgh, and after the service St Martin's choir and staff were presented to them. Commenting on the school being 'singled out for an unscheduled chat with the Queen', a report in a local newspaper said:

> 'Afterwards, when she was due to meet leading members of the SPCK outside, she asked for the girls to be brought outside to meet her too. The school later received a letter from the Queen's secretary, Sir Robert Fellows, referring to "the wonderful choir".'

To mark the school's own tercentenary many activities began to be planned.

The OGA booked St Martin-in-the-Fields Church for a thanksgiving service, and a Charing Cross hotel for a celebratory lunch. The school launched a tercentenary appeal to raise the necessary £450,000 to transform the derelict swimming pool into a sports hall, and to convert the old changing rooms into a drama studio. Although this was described as an ambitious project, it was pointed out that a 300th birthday deserves nothing less.

It came as a surprise to Old Girls, at their AGM, when the forthcoming early retirement of Miss Philpott was announced. Miss Philpott's enthusiasm and dedication to the well-being of the school had resulted in many innovations and the constant reinforcing of standards. The high standards of education and behaviour also meant that each year the school's September intake was vastly over-sub-scribed.

In the newsletter announcing Miss Philpott's retirement, Lady Reid wrote:

'On behalf of all the governors, I wish to express our appreciation for all Miss Philpott has done during the nine marvellous years she has been at St Martin's. We are also delighted that Mrs Morrison, who shares all of Anne Philpott's vision and commitment, has been appointed to succeed her.'

And in describing her time at St Martin's, Miss Philpott said:

'They have been years full of challenge. I have been proud to be part of all the new developments that have taken place and of what is, I believe, a very special school community. . .I am delighted that the Governors have appointed Mrs Lesley Morrison, currently Deputy Head, to be the new Headteacher. She has made a huge contribution to the development of St Martin's over the past seven or so years and will provide the strong leadership the school needs as it faces all the challenges that lie ahead.'

At a reception held at school, Miss Philpott was presented with a 'state-of-the-art' computer — with the hope that many novels would follow! Afterwards, everyone congregated outside the Design and Technology Centre, where they found it had been renamed

The Technology Centre (Siddall)

The Anne Philpott Centre. In a report of the occasion, Mrs Morrison said that the renaming was a permanent reminder of Miss Philpott's time at St Martin's. She added:

> 'As the person succeeding her, I would like to say that it has been a privilege to work with Miss Philpott. I look forward to building on the marvellous legacy she leaves St Martin's, and to taking this very special school community into the twenty-first century.'

Mrs Morrison took over the headship at the start of the summer term. Mr John Chaldcott, previously Head of Science and also married to an Old Girl, became the first male deputy head, with Ms Margaret Hedley continuing as second deputy. In a message to the OGA, Mrs Morrison said:

> 'St Martin's has gone through so many changes, particularly in the last twenty years, that many of you might think the school unrecognisable. We are now a thriving, multi ethnic, inner-city school whose confident, lively and extremely talented pupils are not only well aware of the school's history but are very proud to be part of it . . . As we move towards the next millennium what is the vision for St Martin in the Fields High School for Girls? Firstly, there are certain principles which are not negotiable. Our links with our church and with the SPCK are an immense source of pride and are cherished . . . We also seek to be a forward-looking school where the educational needs of young women in today's society are paramount.'

A few days after her appointment, Mrs Morrison was one of two hundred headteachers and educationalists who were invited to a reception at 10 Downing Street, to celebrate excellence in schools. The government's commitment to education was emphasised, as was the way in which schools would provide a vehicle for social justice.

> 'I thoroughly enjoyed the occasion,' said Mrs Morrison, 'and it was particularly gratifying to talk with other Headteachers and to realise that St Martin's really is at the cutting edge of educational provision.'

The summer term of 1998, like all summer terms, was crowded with activity. Visiting Rochester Castle and Lullington Roman Villa enabled all Year 7 girls to discover many aspects of Roman and Mediaeval history. For Year 8, a visit to the Thames Barrier Exhibition supplemented their work on rivers. Later, they visited Greenwich Park to practise map reading skills.

The following month, fifty-five Year 8 girls visited the Young Vic Theatre to see *Twelfth Night*. Earlier in the day part of the group had a three-hour workshop, with two directors from the Young Vic guiding the girls through different scenes in the play. Drama gained further interest, particularly with Years 8, 9 and 10, through a weekly Drama Club, when leading figures in the theatre ran workshops, watched pupils performing and gave constructive criticism.

Another highlight of the term was when a group of 9 - 13 year olds, from the South African township of Newcastle, captivated the school with traditional Zulu songs and dances. The group travelled the country raising money for a library for their own school, which had classes of over sixty, no equipment and few books. In a flurry of fund-raising, St Martin's girls responded to their needs, competing to see who could raise most money for the group.

When thirteen Year 9 girls entered a competition, organised by the Cabaret Mechanical Theatre, Rebecca O'Neal came third with her automata, Festival of Light. The South East Regional Final was held in the school's Art, Design and Technology Department, and five other St Martin's entrants were commended by the judges.

From over 3,000 entries to the European Multicultural Foundation's essay competition, Akua Accra, in Year 10, came second with her essay *My Vision of a Multicultural Europe*. At the end of June, Akua went to the Royal Commonwealth Club to receive her prize and said:

> 'Martyn Bond, a European Parliament Officer, delivered the opening speech and explained that the theme was 'Multicultural Europe: Strength in Diversity'. Peter Luff, the Director General, then expanded on the theme, followed by Dr Enid Wistrich of Middlesex University who spoke about citizenship and migration. My favourite speaker came later. He was Bob Purkiss, who is a commissioner for the Commission for Racial Equality. He spoke persuasively about race and culture, making important points in a humorous way.'

The following week, Akua Accra went to Woodrow House in Buckinghamshire, where she had previously spent two weeks on work experience. Woodrow House is the home of the London Federation of Clubs for Young People, and on this occasion a new wing was being opened by the Duke of Edinburgh.

After the coach failed to arrive and the bus broke down, the senior gospel choir reached the Queen Elizabeth Hall for the finals of the National Music for Youth Festival. With just time for a hasty change into their gowns, the choir gave 'their usual combination of presence, passion and perfect harmony'. Once again, choirs had come from all over Britain and each waited anxiously for the adjudicators' comments before the presentations. Leigh-Anne Smith, representing St Martin's, was presented with the choir's second Music for Youth Festival certificate.

With a further £22,000 from Accord Energy, another computer network for the Business Studies and IT Centre was installed. This greatly helped the school's link with local primary schools:

> 'The network provides a much needed facility for whole class Information Technology lessons for our local primary schools,' said deputy head Ms Hedley. 'So far, we have welcomed pupils from Holy Trinity and Streatham Wells and are looking forward to inviting more schools in the Autumn term, especially now that Internet access is available.'

In the autumn term, further visits were made by these schools, and also by Brockwell Primary and St Saviour's Primary schools.

Mr Eames, the ICT co-ordinator, not only helped teach the primary school groups computer skills, but trained their teachers too. 'Our next project,' said Mrs Morrison, 'is to run after-school sessions for St Martin's parents.'

Internet and e-mail access were made easier through installing a terminal adaptor, which greatly increased the speed and enabled access through the network on 47 computers.

> 'Staff and students have their own e-mail accounts,' said Mr Segarane, the Network Manager. 'This new technology enables the students to access information from any corner of the world, communicate with students in other schools or countries and create their own web pages on the World Wide Web. This has opened new possibilities in teaching and learning at St Martin's.'

These opportunities were put to good use, by girls in Years 7, 8 and 9 each having an internal e-mail address, while Years 10 and 11 had access through a service provider to 'any on-line computer in the world', There were no significant problems, Mr Eames said, and random checks were made. An after-school club, supervised by teachers, was also started, to give greater confidence in accessing the Internet.

The excitement of increasing technology did not diminish interest in other areas, and in September the steel pan group played the whole afternoon at the West Norwood Fire Service Fete, which 'added greatly to the sunny atmosphere'.

Also in September, an Amnesty International group was formed, with meetings held every three weeks. The group supported a campaign to increase awareness of the Universal Declaration of Human Rights, and two whole-school assemblies were held. They organised a cake stall to raise money, and plans were made to encourage girls and staff to write Christmas cards to be sent to Prisoners of Conscience.

In October, to mark the National Year of Reading and to celebrate Bookweek, the Globe Players visited the school to perform a 'stimulating medley of Shakespeare's best known plays'. Years 7 and 8 watched the excerpts and several girls went on stage to take part. Later in the week, Years 7 and 8 focused on reading across the curriculum, with competitions once more to design a poster advertising a book, write a letter to a favourite author, write a book review or design a book cover.

Fifty members of Year 11 saw an unusual interpretation of *Macbeth*, staged by the Southwark Playhouse. The small auditorium was impressively lit by fifty candles, and the intimate theatre enabled the girls to join in with confidence in the discussion that followed. Their keenness was such that they were described as the 'number one audience'. Afterwards, letters of appreciation from the girls were sent to the Southwark Playhouse.

Another form of discussion took place, one cold November evening, when a group from Year 10 joined the girls of Godolphin and Latymer School. Naomi Moore described the occasion:

'We met the girls at Godolphin and Latymer just in time for the impromptu speeches which involved speaking for one minute about any given subject... We had time for snacks during which we got to know the girls from the host school. Afterwards, we started our formal debate. The proposition was: "This house believes that single sex schools produce more rounded students." The debate went very well and the opposing team had very good points and strong views on why we shouldn't have single sex schools. I was for the motion and ended the debate with a clear conclusion, maintaining that ultimately it doesn't matter if you go to a mixed school or a single sex school, if you want to learn you will learn and if you don't, you won't.'

The debate, chaired by a former president of the Oxford Union, launched a new initiative that paired different types of schools for debates, visits and workshops.

Future events would include joint workshops at both schools, and visits to Oxford, Cambridge and the English Speaking Union to hear 'seasoned debaters'. It was also planned that St Martin's would host a debate with a visiting American team in February.

November had become the month when St Martin's focused on one country, to study the history, geography, religion, art, literature and culture of the people. The chosen country this year was China, and with outside speakers, workshops, research and displays, details of life in China were vividly presented. The month ended with a celebration evening, which included Chinese food, 'dragon' and 'ribbon' dances, poetry and displays, ending with a spectacular display of Kung Fu.

A newsflash in the enlarged *St Martin's News*, produced by the Media Resources Department, stated that for the second year running St Martin's was 'featured in the top 100 state schools in the *Observer* newspaper's listing for December 1998'. This knowledge acted as a further boost for a plan which was coming together, as Mrs Morrison, staff and governors were 'actively investigating the possibility of reopening the 6th Form.'

With the New Year came the exciting prospect of the school's tercentenary. And one great honour was revealed by Mrs Morrison:

'The great news is that Her Majesty the Queen will be visiting the school on February 26th, to help us mark this great milestone in the School's history.'

Planning began, to make the occasion 'in true St Martin's style both memorable and exciting'.

As St Martin's developed, changed and expanded, it didn't forget the early days when, as a simple charity school, it had taken in fifty poor boys and twenty poor girls. From those distant times there had been many educational, economic and social changes. *School* was then a very different place.

The school approaching the 2000s had become a partnership, where students are more responsible for their own path of learning, and the Internet's promised explosion of knowledge is just waiting to be accessed. Even so, reading, composing and communicating are still the vital ingredients that will make sense of this vast store of knowledge.

* * * * *

A stream of laughing, exuberant girls poured through the wide gateway and spilled out on to the pavement in a surge of dark brown school uniforms. The stream spread out as some girls crossed the busy road. Others moved off in both directions, walking down Tulse Hill, singly or in chattering groups.

Uniform prices

	1930s sizes 27-38	**1960s** sizes 30-38	**1990s** sizes 30-46
Blazer	from 20s—33s.9d	75s.9d — £5.5s (badge 9s.6d)	£27 — £37
Blouse	4s.9d — 6s.3d poplin square neck with embroidery	31s.9d — 37s.9d drip-dri with collar	£8.50 — £12.50 short/long sleeves open collar
Tie		7s.11d	
Tunic	17s.11d — 25s	89s.6d — £5.10s	
Skirt		£4.9s.6d — 89s.6d	£12 — £24 machine washable
Cardigan (Bairnswear)		31s.9d — 47s.9d 63s — 89s.6d heavyknit	
Pullover			£14 — £22
Knickers	3s — 4s.3d	5s.9d — 8s.6d	
Winter coat	30s — 40s.6d		
Raincoat		£6.10s — £8.8s	
Velour hat	6s.3d (hatband 2s.9d)	24s.9d	
Panama hat	5s.9d	22s.9d	
PE shirt		19s.11d — 24s.9d	£7.50 — £10.50
PE skirt			£8.99 — £12.50
PE shorts		42s.9d — 45s.9d	
Lycra cycle shorts			£6.99 — £8.50
Socks	3s.11d — 4s.9d		£1.75
Gingham dress		45s.9d — 57s.9d	
Material for dress			5s.6d per yard

On the 1960s uniform list the following were also included:
scarves; swimsuit; indoor and outdoor shoes; hockey boots; white plimsolls.
An interesting comparison can be seen with blazers and blouses in size 34:

Blazer	29s.9d 'A' quality 23s.9d 'B' quality	94s.6d plus badge @ 9s.6d	£32
Blouse	5s.9d	33s.9d	£10.50 long £9.99 short

Bibliography

Betwixt Heaven and Charing Cross: the story of St Martin-in-the-Fields Church by Carolyn Scott, Robert Hale '71

Blackwell Handbook of Education by Farrell, Kerry and Kerry, Blackwell '95

Blazers, Badges and Boaters: a pictorial history of school uniform by Alexander Davidson, Scope '90

Books in Victorian Elementary Schools by Alec Ellis, Library Association '71

Changing Schools. . .Changing Curriculum Ed. Galton and Moon, Harper and Row '83

GCSE; a parent's guide by Allan Matten, Northcote House '88

A Guide to the National Curriculum by Bob Moon, OUP '96

History of Leatherhead by Edwina Vardey, De Valery Co Ltd '88

Multi-Cultural Education: views from the classroom by John Twitchin and Ruth Demuth, BBC '85

A Parents' A-Z of Education by Hilary Mason and Tony Ramsey, Chambers '92

Reluctant Revolutionaries: a century of headmistresses by Mary Price and Nonita Glenday, Pitman '74

A Short History of St Martin-in-the-Fields High School for Girls by D.H. Thomas, 1st edition John Murray '29; part two compiled by M.L. Pearce, 3rd edition '78

A Social History of Education in England by John Lawson and Harold Silver, Methuen '73

Special Educational Needs in Schools by Sally Beveridge, Routledge '93

Storehouse of General Information by Mark Wilks, Cassell 1892

Teaching Technology Ed. Frank Banks, Routledge and OU '94

The Victorian and Edwardian Schoolchild by Pamela Horn, Alan Sutton '89

Willingly to School: a history of women's education by Mary Cathcart Borer, Lutterworth '76

Acknowledgements

My sincere thanks to all who have contributed to this account, including the SPCK, Leatherhead & District Local History Society (L&DLHS) and Old Johnians. Some St Martin's girls and staff have unknowingly contributed by writing for the school magazines and newsletters. Other Old Girls, staff (*) and friends connected with the school (~) have given anecdotes and background details. Maiden names and dates at St Martin's are shown in brackets:-

Michael Ansell (St John's); Daphne Barton (Wood 43-48); Carole Belch (74-84); Judy Bird (42-45); Pearl Bourhill (Gosnel 30-36); Sarah Brooke (Lister 72-79); Marion Campbell (Hardy 40-45); Joan Church (Osmond 43-48); Connie Clarke (Sargent 22-28); Maxine Clarke (Clarke 72-79); James Clube (L&DLHS); Patricia Coe (Denning 40-45); Sylvia Collins (Moakes 45-50); Patricia Cope (Burns 42-45); Adam Darnborough (St John's); Betty Elvy (~Upward); Brenda Fletcher (Mortiboy 26-34); Jennifer Friend (Byers 44-55); Bridget Glanville (Heard 58-64); Mary Gratwick (Marsh 44-53); David Green; Rose Gover (~); Margaret Hamilton (Simmonds 47-52); Mary Harroway (Simmonds 45-51); Jo Hart (~); Phyllis Holmes (Matchin 40-48); Pamela Hough (Ibbott 44-52); Ruth Howe (*78-89); M.J. Hutchings; Margaret Jones (42-47); Janet Kemp (Borrows 53-60); Barbara Lafrance (Nex 29-37); Joan Mangold (*65-78); Joyce Marchant (Gurd 42-50); Christine McCallan (Ireson 48-53); Yvonne McMillar (Hirst 32-43); Philip Morgan (St John's); Eileen Morley (~Baker); Lesley Morrison (*91); Freda Neal (Allen 40-48); Joan Nurse (28-35); Jean Orton (*69-77); Pamela Osborne (Newberry 45-55); Doreen Palmer (Parr 37-42); Barbara Parsons (Hazel Brown 47-53); Margaret Payman (Glen 45-51); Mabel Pearce (*43-71); Anne Philpott (*89-98); Audrey Preston (Newson 37-46); Valerie Punter (Nex 45-48); Janet Redman (*60 -79); Ann Rice-Jones (49-55); Jeanette Ridgeway (Johnson 44-49); Jenny Russell (Taylor 42-52); Jeanne Scotzin (Austin 28-35); Kate Sidell (Lister 76-81); Freda Smith (44-41); Ruth Smith (~); Ann Walker (~); Jean Walton (Hey 32-45); Sheila Watt (Atkins 47-56); Susanne Weston (Mico 80-86); Josephine Williams (Brown 31-42); Joyce Wright (*58-78).

Finally, many thanks to Nigel Green, Robin Rowe and Jane Stevens for their much valued comments and suggestions.

Index

Absenteeism, 28, 178
Accord Energy, 192, 204
Acts - Education, 115, 159, 174, 175
  Elementary Education, 32
  Endowed Schools, 33
  General Workhouse, 22
Air raid shelters, 86, 89-90, 104, 108
America, 68, 70, 106, 121, 121, 163, 181, 195
American, 103, 131-132, 206
Apprenticeship, 17-18
Association of Headmistresses, 37
Athletics, 119, 147, 154, 170, 186-187, 196
Australia/n, 52, 70, 132
Austria, 79, 154
BBC, 70, 121, 131, 133, 151, 193
Beating the Bounds, 25
Behaviour, 10, 15, 16, 25, 53, 54, 57, 73,
  166, 180, 200
Belgium, 76
Board schools, 32-33, 41
Bombing, 43, 86, 89, 90, 100, 106, 108, 110
  111
Bulgaria, 167
Bullying, 185
Buss, Francis Mary, 36, 37
Camberwell, 122, 125, 162, 179, 193
Canada/ian, 53, 68, 70, 102, 115, 131, 185
Careers, 79, 165, 196
Caretakers, 61, 86, 148
Carol Service, 133, 145, 164, 168
Carroll, Lewis, 57
Charity children, 13-34
Charity collections, 47
Child labour, 33, 40, 45
Choir, 72, 133, 146, 167, 179, 193, 197, 200
Citizenship, 105-6, 121, 126, 149
Clubs and societies, 12, 66, 72, 91, 105,
  115-6, 140, 144, 156-8 170, 195, 203, 205
Comic Relief, 188
Comprehensive Ed., 124, 158, 164, 166,
  168
Computer, 169, 170, 178, 185

Conscience clause, 33
Cornwall, 154, 177
Cricket, 42, 64
Cycling, 39, 60, 91, 92, 97
Davies, Emily, 33, 46
Denmark, 31, 121
Design Council, 182
Devon, 149
Dig for Victory, 91
Discipline, 19, 25, 41, 72, 104, 157, 163,
  166
Duke of Edinburgh Award, 149-150, 170,
  195
English Speaking Union, 151, 163, 206
Enrichment Courses, 162
Equal Opportunities Group, 191
Evacuation, 81-111
Examinations -
  CSE, 152, 168, 170-172
  Eleven plus, 124, 159
  Music, 51, 132, 150
  GCE, 132, 134, 141,152, 161, 163, 165,
    168, 171-172, 178
  GCSE, 171-172, 174, 181, 191, 193, 195,
    197, 199
  GSC, 46, 73, 88, 94, 99, 107-110, 132
  Royal Society of Arts, 73
  Secretarial, 74, 141
  University locals, 32, 46
Exhibitions -
  Britain Can Make It, 122
  British Empire, 53
  Electron Jubilee, 125
  Eurotunnel, 186
  Ideal Home, 161
  Indian/Pakistani Art, 125
  LCC Education, 134
  Living in Lambeth, 143
  Pompeii, 161
  St Martin's Church, 158
  Thames Barrier, 202
  Young Artists/Designers, 172

Fashion show, 145,179
Festival of Britain, 133-134
Festival of Youth, 53
Field studies, 149, 155, 156, 168, 169, 188, 195, 202
Fitness for Life, 170
Flags, 45, 50, 75
Founders' Day, 75-76, 78, 113, 128, 145, 157, 168, 190
France, 40, 43, 44, 70, 108, 115, 156, 186, 190
Funding, 10, 16, 24, 30 31, 173, 181
Further education, 124, 178
Gardening, 67, 69, 91, 97
General election, 76
General strike, 49-50
Germany, 77, 79, 127, 136
Gilbert and Sullivan, 145, 161, 167
Girl Guides, 96
Grant Maintained status, 182
Harvest camp, 103, 110
Hitler Youth, 77
Hockey, 42, 48, 71, 72, 94, 147, 166
Holland, 77, 127
Homework, 66, 120, 157, 178, 180
Houses of Parliament, 51, 52, 106, 123
Humphry Essay Prize, 102
ILEA, 149, 165, 171, 172
Industrial Revolution, 25, 32
Industrial schools, 21, 28
Infant School Society, 29
International Museum Week, 141-142
Internet, 204, 207
IT, 178, 192, 204
Jubilee, 129, 130-131
Kent, 66, 110, 189
Key Stages, 178, 182, 183
Knitting, 13, 15, 22, 27, 81, 97
LCC, 41, 61, 77, 79, 81-82, 88, 99, 124, 134, 144, 149
League of Nations, 53, 67
Library, 25, 60, 61, 86, 98, 157, 169, 171, 178, 198, 203
Locke, John, 10
Lost property, 47, 69
Meals, 26, 31-32, 40, 42, 66, 73, 139-140,

186, 191, 195
Minibus, 166
Monitorial system, 28
Music Centre, 192
National Bookweek, 169, 198, 205
National Curriculum, 13, 174, 178, 182, 189
National Festival of Music, 197, 204
National Savings, 98, 102
National schools, 32
Netball, 42, 44, 58, 69, 72, 94
Newspapers -
   Brixton Free Press, 116
   Church Times, 199
   Daily Advertiser, 27
   Daily Express, 52
   Daily Telegraph, 130
   Morning Herald, 27
   Observer, 206
   South London Press, 131
   Times, 27, 130
   West Norwood Times, 116
Ofsted, 194-195
OGA, 105, 176, 200, 202
Orchestra, 65, 132, 150, 172,179
Parents Assoc./PSFA, 120, 125, 148, 169, 170, 174, 175, 184, 185
PE/Gym, 41, 59, 70, 90, 118, 119, 120, 134, 145, 162, 168, 170, 176
Picard Prof, 76
Picnics, 45, 48, 92, 102, 158
Poetry, 51, 57, 67, 97, 148, 190, 198
Posture Stripe, 117-118
Primary education, 125, 178, 204
Prize Day, 39, 120-121, 168
PSHE, 168, 172, 198
Pupil-teacher, 28, 36
Queen Mother, 62, 130
Quiet room, 166
Radio/wireless, 70
Ragged schools, 29
Rationing, 43, 81, 85 , 122, 139
Readathon, 176, 179
Red Cross, 91, 94, 103
Road Safety, 149

Royal Society, 137
Russia, 101, 106, 152
Salvage, 98, 102
SATs, 182, 198
School - Boards, 32, 41
  Council, 74, 105, 118, 120, 171, 185-186
  Cruise, 159-160
  Doctor , 114
  Houses, 45, 46, 47, 48, 50, 52, 69, 70
  Inspections, 33, 40, 79, 137
  Leaving age, 33, 40, 45, 156
  Medicals, 114
School locations -
  Charing Cross Road , 35-56
  George Street, 26, 27
  Heming's Row, 27, 29, 35, 38
  Hungerford Market House, 14, 21, 25
  Hunts Court, 17, 18
  Leatherhead, 81-112
  Silwood House, 43, 48, 51, 86, 145, 166,
    199
  Tulse Hill, 13, 43, 45, 48, 50-51, 55, 56,
    57-207
Schools and Colleges -
  Academy of Boys Edinburgh, 151,
  Alleyn's, 161, 167
  Archbishop Tenison, 39, 40, 133
  Blind School Hospital, 94
  Brockwell Primary, 204
  Burlington, 44
  Cardiff Boys', 151
  Chatham County, 76
  Cheltenham Ladies' College, 33
  Christ's Hospital, 35
  City of Bath, 151
  City of London, 117
  Clapham County, 154
  Clapham Secondary, 117
  Clear View, 71
  Crewe Girls', 151
  Dick Sheppard, 143, 154, 155, 168,171
  Diocesan Training College, 38
  Dorking County, 94
  Dorking Grammar, 92
  Dulwich College, 113

Emmanuel, 151
Francis Holland, 44
Godolphin and Latymer, 205-206
Grey Coat, 35, 44, 70, 117
Guildford High, 101
Haberdasher Aske's, 80, 86
Holy Trinity, 204
James Allen, 66, 80, 94, 101, 117, 151,
  166
La Retraite, 117, 154
Mary Datchelor, 67, 123, 154
Marylebone High, 42
Merton Abbey, 71
Midhurst Grammar, 77
North London Collegiate, 36
Northampton Girls', 66
Oakfield, 149
Parson's Mead, 95
Peckham Secondary, 71
Queen's College, 36, 37
Red Maids', 35
Rosebery County, 95
Secondary English Language, 167
St Andrew's Convent, 90
St Clement's, 25
St Dunstan's, 25
St Hugh's Oxford, 99
St John's, 81-113
St Jude's, 179, 200
St Saviour's, 204
Strand, 86, 92, 113, 127, 155
Streatham College, 71
Streatham County, 70, 76, 117
Streatham High, 107
Streatham Hill, 71
Streatham Wells, 204
Sutton High, 95
Sydenham High, 117
Thurlow Park, 162
Toynbee Hall School of Drama, 120
Tulse Hill Boys', 151, 168
University College, 95
Uppingham, 37
Van Steuben High, 131
Wantage High, 136

Wimbledon High, 154
Woodford High, 136
Secondary education, 35, 37, 41, 124-125
Shakespeare Memorial Company, 68
Shropshire, 149, 183
Skiing, 154-155, 156, 170
SPCK, 10, 14, 17, 18, 21, 28, 30, 143, 173,
    190, 200, 202
Special-needs, 180
Sports Day, 50, 64, 119, 196-197
Steel band, 179, 192-193
Surrey, 66, 71-72, 110, 158
Sussex, 66, 110, 174
Swimming pool, 95, 119, 129, 131, 144,
    147, 153, 161, 166, 182, 187, 190, 200
Switzerland, 170
Teacher training, 13, 35, 105, 115, 150
Technology Centre, 182, 187, 189, 192,
    201, 204
Television, 143, 144, 160, 169, 177, 180,
    185, 188, 197, 199, 203
Tennis, 72, 92, 93, 94, 97, 136, 170
Theatre, 42, 43, 52, 67, 68, 106, 122, 125,
    163, 168, 187, 197, 198, 203, 205
Thring, Dr Edward, 37
Timetable, 74, 88, 99, 168
Top of the Form, 151
Trinity 6th form, 168
Tripartite system, 124
Tutorial classes, 88
Uniform, 15, 40, 41, 58, 85, 86, 88, 136, 148,
    153, 157, 164, 166, 180, 183-184
Video, 160, 172, 180
Visual aids, 160-161
Wales/Welsh, 44, 156, 177, 197
Walking, 30-31, 50, 91, 97, 166
Wiltshire, 103
Women's Lib, 155, 156
Work experience, 161, 168, 194, 196, 203
World War 1, 43, 44, 61, 199
World War 2, 81-111
WVS, 83, 85, 97, 112, 136
Yorkshire, 149
Young Citizen of the Year, 188

Abbreviations:

ARP	Air Raid Precautions
ATs	Attainment Targets
CEWC	Council for Education and World Citizenship
CSE	Certificate of Secondary Education
DES	Department of Education and Science
ERA	Education Reform Act
GCE	General Certificate of Education
GCSE	General Certificate of Secondary Education
GSC	General Schools Certificate
LEA	Local Education Authority
GLC	Greater London Council
ILEA	Inner London Education Authority
IT	Information Technology
LCC	London County Council
NRA	National Record of Achievement
NVQ	National Vocational Qualification
OGA	Old Girls' Association
OFSTED	Office for Standards in Education
PSFA	Parents, Staff, Friends Association
PSHE	Personal, Social and Health Education
PT/PE	Physical Training/Education
SATs	Standard Attainment Tasks
SPCK	Society for Promoting Christian Knowledge
SEAC	Schools Examination and Assessment Council
TVEI	Technical, Vocational and Educational Initiative
UNA	United Nations Association
UNO	United Nations Organisation
UNESCO	United Nations Educational, Scientific and Cultural Organisation
USSR	Union of Soviet Socialist Republics
VAD	Voluntary Aid Detachment
WVS	Women's Voluntary Service